7 FIGURE RETIREMENT

REAL ESTATE INVESTING STRATEGIES FOR IMMIGRANTS

LURLINE HENRIQUES
TT&T PROPERTIES INC.

ISBN-13: 978-1512159479
ISBN-10: 1512159476

PUBLISHED BY:
10-10-10 PUBLISHING
MARKHAM, ON
CANADA

Contents

Foreword

There is an African proverb that says "Smooth seas do not make skillful sailors." It's why I think it's so important to get your advice from people who've faced big challenges in life and triumphed. It's also why I am so excited for you to meet and learn from Lurline. I meet so many people every day in my business and it's rare but such a pleasure when I meet someone like Lurline who has so much passion for helping others by sharing her expertise and experience.

Not satisfied with the options she had in Jamaica, Lurline made the brave decision at the young age of 21 to leave her home country in search of a better life with more opportunity. At first, she had to work hard just to get an education so she could get a good job, then she worked very hard to raise her three professional daughters while working full time with the Federal Government. She again worked very hard to ensure her and her family's future by investing the money she could save in real estate.

Ten years later, investing with hard work, honesty and integrity, she's looking at a very comfortable seven figure retirement and wants you to know that it's possible for you too - even if you're a new immigrant to Canada faced with cultural and financial challenges right now.

Her goal with this book is to help you cut through the hype and learn the key strategies that brought her the greatest gains. She also wants all immigrants in Canada to move upward in achieving wealth, and one of the best ways to do this is by investing in real estate. She shares simplified strategies that everyone will be able to enjoy, understand and follow.

It's exciting for me to introduce her to you as she has a burning desire to see more immigrants take more risks in real estate investing because it is only then that they will achieve wealth. There is no limit to what can be achieved in Canada.

After reading this excellent book, I highly recommend it to anyone seeking clear advice to invest in real estate, especially people who are not originally from Canada. I think you'll relate to her stories and appreciate her key tips to helping you take advantage of your culture and Canadian home. I look forward to hearing about your 7 Figure Retirement!

RAYMOND AARON
New York times Bestselling Author and
Founder of The Raymond Aaron Group

Introduction

Welcome to *7 Figure Retirement*; I am glad you found me. Congratulations on taking the first step toward building a solid, profitable real estate portfolio. The strategies described in this book will move you forward in achieving your real estate retirement goals. Whether you are a novice or seasoned investor you will benefit from the lessons throughout each chapter.

While there are numerous theoretically based real estate books published, very few demonstrate how ordinary people, especially immigrants, really make money with real estate; what were the steps that they took; how did they get from point A to point B and so forth. Most also do not show you how to avoid hurdles.

Many people including myself have spent thousands of dollars on real estate education, going from course to course and from seminar to seminar and that's it. Once you leave the course and the seminar there is no more encouragement, no more enthusiasm, no more motivation and therefore no real estate investing. The moment I realized the strategies in making 7 figures, I told myself that I should help others to attain the same goal - so here I am!

After you have read this book you will be motivated to become a successful, sophisticated real estate investor. The reason is that you will be taught how to invest in your greatest asset and that is "you". Successful people know that this is the only asset that can never be lost. According to Forbes list, the five wealthiest people in the world are: Bill Gates, Carlos Slim Helu, Amancio Ortega, Warren Buffett and Larry Ellison; and what do these men all have in common you might ask? They all invested to some extent in real estate! I hope by now you are convinced that real estate investing can make you millions if you know how.

Please relax, get comfortable and enjoy the journey in the following chapters of this book. I am about to show you how to cut through all the sales pitches, theories, hypes and myths that surrounds real estate investing. Just bear in mind that the ABSOLUTE best way to find success as a real estate investor is to create a plan...and FOLLOW IT!

Over ten years ago my husband's company downsized and he was presented with a package because he was one of the employees at the top of the salary scale. It was quite disastrous because our daughters had already started studying in the United States and the tuition was quite expensive. Being a spiritual person I communicated with the Lord and inquired of Him what to do? He revealed to me that the best thing for me was to leave my comfortable Federal Government job and become self-employed, at which time I could earn as much as I wanted.

The entrepreneurial spirit was always in me as a child so I had no further questions to ask the Lord. I immediately negotiated with my union at work and was able to trade a package with someone whose job was affected by government cuts. It was very difficult to convince my husband because he thought it was really bad timing. However, I was able to persuade him that it was what I wanted to do and I thought it was the best thing for us at the time. He finally gave me the go-ahead.

At the time I was qualified to open a paralegal practice, specializing in Immigration, Pensions and Worker's Compensation, so that's what I did. I was making enough money to get by, combined with my husband's new salary but after a while I was not satisfied with my level of achievement. At the close of each day I would do research into other types of businesses; make inquiries; read books; attend seminars and workshops, etc. etc. One of the books that I found was *Rich Dad Poor Dad* by Robert Kiyosaki. Well, this was quite aspiring so I kept digging deeper and deeper into what he was teaching. I actually inquired about his courses but they were out of my price range since we had daughters who were high achievers and were heading for studies in the United States. I enrolled into other real estate investment courses – ones that I could afford - and made the best of them.

Unfortunately these courses were presented by U.S. presenters with U.S. strategies, which are not exactly the same as in Canada. Nevertheless, during all of these courses the main phrase that I took away and that most people took away was "take action." I had met another lady who had the same interest as I had so we decided to drive around in different areas looking for properties so that we could "take action". We came upon a lovely 9-plex which contained 8 two-bedroom apartments and 1 one-bedroom apartment. Everything seemed fine, the building looked good, the price sounded right, it generated enough rent to pay the bills and all that good stuff so I decided to "take action". This building was exactly one hour from my front door. I rushed home with excitement and told my husband that I found a property." I sat at the table, unfolded all the information but at the end of my conversation he did not share my excitement. Of course he does not have the same passion as I do, so why would he be excited? Fortunately he is someone who I can reason with so he gave me his approval to start negotiating; "Thank you Lord" I said. Now please pay attention to what transpired from here on; remember, I am anxious to "take action". My friend introduced me to a residential real estate agent. I was told that she was very honest, worked with integrity, had several years of experience and she would be good for me. I did a bit of research on her and was satisfied with my findings and therefore decided to hire her. What I did not know at the time was that I was purchasing a commercial building and therefore I should have been working with a commercial agent and not a residential agent.

I did my due diligence on the building and the area and decided to put an offer on the property. This agent completed the offer and set the closing date to be 30 days from the date of the offer, as she would normally do with a residential property. She further instructed me to present a $50,000 cheque with the offer. I explained to her that I did not have $50,000 in my chequing account and she told me that the office would hold the cheque and it would not be negotiated until a few days prior to closing.

A day after I submitted the offer I got a call from the real estate broker stating that the funds were not in the bank. I told him that I explained to the agent that the funds were not in the chequing account and she told me that I did not need to have them at that particular time. The broker then said I must have misunderstood what the agent told me because the funds were required immediately.

This was my first disappointing and upsetting news because I had to prematurely close our GIC account, and lost the interest, in order to make the $50,000 payment.

The next upsetting news came when we realized that we would never be able to close this deal in 30 days because we required an environmental study and the process was quite lengthy.

One week prior to closing my agent requested a 30 day extension; by that time the vendor's agent realized that my agent was not experienced in this area, so he gave an additional 15 days instead of the requested 30, which was still not sufficient.

At the end of the 45 days the process was still incomplete. The bank told us verbally that the deal was going to be alright; however they had to wait for some other documentation which would take at least another week. In order for us not to lose our $50,000 deposit, we had to do some bridge financing in the interim which cost us a few thousand unnecessary dollars. If only we had the right agent in the first place this would not have happened.

So many things went wrong on our first deal that some people wonder why I am still doing real estate investing. I tell people that I am still doing it because it is my passion and I knew that I was determined to continue until I got to my destination. I was always told as a child not to look at the journey when I was pursuing my dreams, but to stay focused on the destination, so that's what I did. I also remembered the words of Conrad Hilton who said "Success seems to be connected with action. Successful people keep moving. They make mistakes, but they don't quit." I look at people like Donald Trump; how many mistakes he made, how many times he filed bankruptcy. He keeps on going, so why shouldn't I and why shouldn't you?

I am explaining this simple error that occurred in our first deal, an error that had cost us an extra $10,000, hoping that it will be a learning tool for you so that you will not make the same mistake. Be sure to hire people who are experienced in the field that you are pursuing. Be sure to hire the right agent and the right lawyer. If my book says that something is possible, it really is possible. Likewise, if someone tells you that it cannot be done just move on and inquire of someone else. There are accountants and brokers who are not familiar with creative financing so find those who are familiar.

This book is based on my experience - as an immigrant - in real estate investing. I am pointing out my mistakes so that you can avoid them and the tools that I used to make the journey shorter and more profitable. I am not saying that real estate investing is for everyone but I am saying if you try it and you like it, it can be a money machine if it's done correctly. If you make a mistake, do not quit; just use it as a learning tool and continue on your journey.

Find an inspiring mentor. That person does not have to meet with you face to face. I read Robert Kiyosaki's *Rich Dad Poor Dad* and I made him my mentor. Frankly, I have paid other people to mentor me and they ran off after two meetings. I have never met Robert Kiyosaki but when I read his book I called him my mentor and I tried to emulate him in small ways. You can do the same. Find someone who you admire for their success in the real estate business and let them motivate you by their achievements. My hope is that this book will also motivate you as you go through the various chapters.

In the last couple years I have done more in real estate investing than I did in the first eight years. This book will show you the tools that I have used in the last two years and if you follow them you too will achieve your 7 Figure Retirement in the near future. While at first it may seem important that you learn everything you can about real estate investing, in reality it is best to focus on two things: an investment vehicle and a strategy for using that vehicle. Once you read this book, discover what part of this industry ignites your passion, work on it, stay focused and keep repeating the process until you reach your goal. Remember not to focus on the journey, just the destination and you will be successful. If I can do it as an immigrant in this country, so can you!

Japanese Proverb states: "Fall seven times - stand up eight."

Chapter One
Why Should You Invest in Real Estate?

First and Foremost

The main reason you should invest in real estate is because it is a wealth creation tool that can take you to your 7 Figure Retirement. You must define, however, where you want real estate investment to take you financially. If you do not know where you would like to go, you will not be able to foresee where I am taking you; if you cannot foresee where I am taking you, you will never get there.

There are two concepts that are mentioned regularly in the successful investing world. Those concepts are diversification and asset allocation. Both of these involve spreading your investments around to mitigate risk while trying to get a higher return than might be achieved with safer investments. Real estate is often mentioned as a portion of a well diversified portfolio. There are several strategies in real estate investing that I will explain in a later chapter.

When you own and operate a real estate investment business, you are in a position to do something that almost no other investment offers. Namely, to reap higher than average returns with lower than average risk.

Before I get into the reasons, let me define very specifically what type of real estate investment I mean and what type I do not. There are three characteristics that must exist to meet my definition of high return/low risk real estate investing.

1. You own property directly or have an ownership interest in specific properties.
2. That property produces a regular income that exceeds your expenses.

3.   You provide some level of labor or management necessary to run this as a business rather than as a pure investment.

We can look at a rental property, for example,

Depending on the size of the property, it can be purchased with 5% down and in some instances with no money down, depending on your creativity, which we will get to in chapter 8. While the renters are paying down your mortgage, your property is increasing in equity and at the same time you are gaining cash flow each month, which means that your income stream will also be growing over time. (This depends of course on how and where you purchased the property). All of these act as a hedge against inflation. Unlike the more typical items offered as inflation hedges such as gold, real estate gives you income while you wait. Gold just sits there.

Income Stream Is Passive

Real estate is known to be far more passive than running a traditional business. (If you are a novice investor and not sure what passive income is, it is an income received on a regular basis, with little effort required to maintain it). If you hire outside management it will reduce your income stream somewhat, but it can then be even more passive. It is important to note, however, that it should never be 100% passive. If you have no idea what is going on with your business, you have lost the safety buffer the business is designed to provide. The income stream it produces tends to be extremely stable and predictable. Rents tend to rise over time and even during tough economic times they tend to be fairly stable. You won't find yourself wondering how much income your properties will produce next year. They should produce higher than they produced last year with the increase in rent or property expansion. If they don't, they are being poorly managed and this must be addressed.

Rental properties, when purchased correctly, generate significant cash flow. If purchased with 100% cash, the cash flow is going to approximate the cap rate and that rate tends to run approximately 12% depending on the type of property and where we are in the real estate cycle. Currently many properties are able to produce numbers near the high end of that range or even above it. These are very strong numbers. Remember that this doesn't take into account the appreciation of the property. This is just cash that you put into your pocket every year; cash that is not all taxable due to deprecation; cash that will be generated reliably year after year with no significant reduction, but slow consistent increases. If the property is purchased with 20% down the approximate cap rate can be 8% and higher, again depending on the area of purchase.

The cash flow a property generates is the single most important thing about real estate investing. If an era of real estate investing offered no properties that could generate good cash flow, such as in the early 2000's, I would simply not be a buyer of any additional real estate in that environment. Keep in mind, however, that properties you already own will continue to perform as they always have, regardless of the inability of new properties to do so.

The reason this is so critically important is because it is why real estate investing can be both stable and low risk. Refusing to buy properties that do not offer strong cash flow will keep you out of investment trouble. There is no shortage of people who have lost a lot of money investing in real estate, but not people who had properties that were generating significant cash flow. I cannot stress this enough. Successful, safe real estate investing revolves around cash flow. You should never purchase properties with appreciation as your primary objective. Your business runs on cash and cash flow, not on appreciation. It is so important that it can almost be your only measure of success and safety. Cash flow is king!

Freedom of Time

Time is money; it's also one of the few things in life that can't be replaced once it's gone. Real estate allows you freedom to enjoy your life while your properties are appreciating and providing you with cash flow.

One of the first things I will teach you as an immigrant investor is to create your business plan and then create an action plan. Remember you must change your actions in order to change your results.

Your business plan will save you time because it will help you to avoid big mistakes. The last thing you want to do is work on your start-up for a year, only to realize you were doomed to fail from the start. Many real estate investors learn the hard way; they did not have enough money and did not seek out how to allocate additional funds prior to starting the business, or they took on partners with the wrong skills and resources. Developing and sharing a business plan can help ensure that you're sprinting down the right path.

Your business plan will help make you into a real estate investor and not a speculator. Your emotions should be counter-balanced. At times during your start-up experience, you'll be manic; so passionate about your ideas you lose sight of reality. At other times, you'll be overwhelmed by doubt, fear, or exhaustion. When your emotions get the best of you, having a business plan lets you step back, and take an objective look at what you are doing and why, what you know for a fact and what you are trying to figure out.

Your business plan will make sure everyone is on the same page if you are working with partners in order to launch your business faster and smarter. Ideally, you'll have partners, so you can launch faster, smarter, and with less need to pay employees or suppliers. Even if you don't have partners, you may have family, friends, and advisers involved. A business plan helps get everyone involved in your start-up, heading in the same direction.

Your business plan will act as a game plan or action plan. At start-up, execution is everything. That means you have to set priorities, establish goals, and measure performance. You also need to identify the key questions to answer, like "What features do customers really want?"

"Will customers buy or rent our properties (depending on your exit strategy) and how much will they pay?" and "How can we attract customers in a way that's cost effective and scalable?" These are all things you'll address during the business planning process.

Your business plan will indicate how you will raise capital. If you raise or borrow money - even from friends and family - you'll need to communicate your vision in a clear, compelling way. A good business plan will help you do just that. A business with a business plan will raise twice as much capital as a business without.

Your action plan on the other hand, will be focusing on where you want real estate investment to take you financially. Be specific about how this success looks; for example;

- How will you be spending your time?
- What exactly will your financial picture look like?
- Will you continue to work in your field or will you live off the cash flow from your properties?

As with any successful journey, you need to know where you are going in order to get there, and that destination needs to be very specific. Set a realistic timeframe in which to achieve this success. Ask yourself:

- How long do I realistically believe it will take me to get there?
- What buffer time do I have in case of unforeseen detours?
- Will I be disappointed if I get to my financial destination later than expected?
- How will I feel if I get there earlier than expected?

The key is to be realistic and remember that proper real estate investing will create long-term wealth.

Leverage

If you don't over-leverage your real estate investments, they will make you wealthy. One of the greatest advantages of investing in real estate is your ability to use leverage. In finance, leverage is a general term for any technique to multiply gains and losses. In real estate, leverage allows you to achieve a much higher return on investment than you could without it. Real estate investing allows you to use leverage when you buy. It allows you to use it when you operate. It also allows you to use it across multiple tenants. Using leverage in your real estate investments can have a big effect on your financial statement.

More than any other alternative investment, real estate is designed to take advantage of leverage. Can you imagine what your banker would say if you came in and told him, "I want to purchase $1,000,000 worth of XYZ Company's stock. Will you finance 80% of it and I'll bring 20% to the closing table?" Most likely, the banker would laugh and politely ask you to exit his office. However, that is exactly what bankers agree to every day when making loans to real estate investors.

When I first started in real estate investing, a wise investor told me "If you use leverage to your advantage, it will make you very wealthy. However, if you over-leverage (take out too large a loan) on your properties, you will lose them." I think that advice still rings true. If you use financing responsibly you will be rewarded. The properties will produce positive cash flow and grow in value. However, if you take on too large a loan on your properties and take all your money out, you run a high risk of losing them. Taking a larger loan than your properties can support can cause them to no longer produce positive cash flow if the market goes down.

Let's take a quick look at how leverage can be used successfully in real estate investing. It is used three ways in real estate to create wealth and massive income:

Financing Your Purchase

Real estate is one of the few places that if you buy something for $100,000, you need only a small fraction of the purchase price. As an immigrant, the banks will still lend you a significant percentage of the purchase price. They will finance it and allow you to pay them back over time. Buying real estate using financing allows you to control more properties than you could if you paid all cash. For example, if you had $150,000 to invest, you could buy a duplex for all cash (no loan) that produces $12,000 a year in income. However, if you take the same $150,000 and use leverage, you can buy property valued at as much as $750,000. If the bigger property generates $6,000 a month in income and you subtract the loan payment of $4,000, you would make $2,000 a month. That is double what you would have made without using financing. By financing your purchase, you would be able to buy a bigger property. That bigger property could produce more income and increased your return on investment.

Income Property Valuation

Investment real estate is valued by the income that it generates after subtracting expenses. So, if you raise income or lower expenses, you raise the income and value of the property. If you do both, it raises the value and cash flow even more. Depending on the property, this can increase the value 10- or even 12-fold. For example, an increase in income or a decrease in expenses of $10,000 in a year could increase the value of your property by as much as $100,000 -$140,000. Small changes to the performance of the property over time can make you huge amounts of money.

Multiple Tenant Principle

Investment in real estate with multiple tenants allows you to use leverage; real estate like an apartment complex, office building, or retail center.   You can maximize your return by making small adjustments across multiple tenants, such as small adjustments in rent. With one apartment it doesn't make much difference to your income. However, when applied across multiple tenants, small changes can add up to create big results. For instance, let's say you own a 100 unit apartment complex. If you raise rents $10 per month, per unit, you actually create $1,000 a month in extra income. Just imagine what happens when one day you have 1,000 apartment units. You make the same $10 rent increase, but this time it increases your income by $10,000 per month. By making small adjustments across multiple tenants it can increase your investment dramatically.

As you can see, leverage is one of the biggest advantages to investing in real estate. As long as you use it responsibly and avoid taking on loans that are too big for your properties, it can be your greatest asset or, it can be accentuated by making small changes in income or expenses over time. These changes can dramatically increase your income and net worth.

Chapter Two
Legal Immigrants

Are You A Legal Immigrant to Canada?

If you are and you're feeling nervous about investing in Canada, let me assure you that you should be excited, not fearful.

The opportunities for you to create real estate wealth in this country are limitless, whether you were born here or not.

Arriving in Canada at the age of 21, I was all alone. I had no family here. A couple friends encouraged me to come to Canada as they knew that I was in search of other prospects. I did some research on the country and felt that it was a good place to live.

Even though I was living in Kingston, the capital city of Jamaica, it was a tough place to be. My family was there but the opportunities to make a good living were limited. I knew I needed to make a change or the cycle would just keep repeating itself and my kids would be born without opportunity as well.

The processing of the paperwork was easy...the decision to move was not. Within three months from the date of the application I had my police record and medical completed, my visa and social insurance number were in my hands.

Being at such young age and having no family in this country, I was excited to immigrate but at the same time I was fearful because I had no idea what to expect. Even before I landed from the plane I looked out the window and became paralyzed with fear. I began to ask myself if I had done the right thing. The streets were so wide, compared to our little streets. The cars were rushing back and forth and the radiance from the lights on the light poles was so dazzling that I remembered saying to myself, "Oh my Lord." Even though I was a driver back home, the fact that these streets were so wide and the driving was on the right side of the road, while I would drive on the left in Jamaica, took some adaptation.

Immigrating to Canada was the start of a new life for me. I cannot say it was easy; however, I knew what I wanted so I stayed focused. The first thing that I did was find a job. I was alone here so I knew that the rent had to be paid, and therefore I had to find a job before the money that I brought ran out. Within the first couple days after my arrival I went for four interviews, and was offered all four jobs, because I was a very good short-hand writer and those were the days for short-hand secretaries. I chose the job that was best for me, and I worked extremely hard and diligent so that they would have no regrets hiring me, and it went really well. At nights I would go home and cry myself to sleep because of loneliness but in the morning I would be ready to go and follow my daily routine.

Coming from a Christian home I knew that it was important to plant myself in a church because the Bible teaches that those who plant themselves in the house of the Lord will flourish in the courts of our God. I wanted to flourish in the courts of our God so I found myself a church and made a family out of the church members. I tried to do all that I could to take my mind off my family and friends that I left behind. I knew that I had to do so if I wanted to grow in this unfamiliar country with unfamiliar personalities.

My next mission was to register at the university to continue my studies that I interrupted in order to immigrate to this beautiful country. By this time I was quite busy with work, school and church. My days of crying were over and I was gradually getting settled.

Most people who leave their home country and immigrate to a foreign land experience culture shock, defined as the feeling of disorientation, insecurity, anxiety, unfamiliar surroundings, unfamiliar behaviors, loneliness, and the list goes on and on. However, if you tell yourself that you are not alone and think of a positive reason why you immigrated, that feeling will soon disappear.

If you are an immigrant, I am glad you are reading this book, especially this chapter, because you can ask yourself, "if this little Jamaican lady can make such a remarkable difference in her life, why can't I?" I raised three professional daughters while achieving my goals, even without social media. If I could do it then, why can't you do it now?

You can use social media to connect with the globe and maximize your income:

Facebook

Even though Facebook, a social networking website, was originally designed for college students, today there are more than one billion users worldwide, connecting and sharing with family and friends online. It is the largest social network.

A Facebook page has many potential benefits for any business, but one of the main benefits you will find is that it will increase your sales and profits.

You can use Facebook as a low cost marketing strategy: Marketing activities that would cost thousands of dollars through other channels can be done on Facebook for a fraction of the cost. This makes it ideal for small to medium businesses with a limited marketing budget. Larger businesses can also market their concepts through Facebook before committing to bigger and more expensive advertising.

You can share basic information such as your business name, address and contact details, and a brief description of your products and services. You can also post pictures and videos about your business, which is a powerful way to communicate with customers and potential customers and allow them to see your product or service without having to visit your premises.

You can use Facebook to talk to existing and potential customers by posting and receiving messages. Be mindful to only share information that is useful and interesting to other users.

Facebook can raise brand awareness and promote positive word-of-mouth. You can increase your business's profile by encouraging existing and potential customers to click the 'Like' button on your Facebook page. Once they like your page, your customers will receive your updates on their wall where their friends will also see them. This helps to build awareness of your business and to associate their friends with your brand.

Facebook can steer traffic to your website. You can include a link to your website on your Facebook page. Many businesses report that the greatest benefit of Facebook is the extra traffic that it steers to their site. Visitors who come to the website can be exposed to stronger marketing messages and, often, the option of buying goods and services.

Communicating with your clients or fans over Facebook sounds friendly in theory, but some people may use your Facebook page as a venue to write offensive comments or post spam. A user might even post false allegations about your business on your page for anyone to see. As a result, your business needs to be monitoring its Facebook page frequently, ideally checking each individual post.

Do not use Facebook to aggressively promote your products or services. You'll have much greater success if you share information related to your business that is actually useful or interesting to other users. This increases your credibility and promotes your business by building long-term relationships with other users.

You should also listen as much as you talk. Paying attention to what the market thinks about your business, your industry, a product or a marketing campaign can provide valuable insights.

Twitter

This is micro-blogging. Twitter and 'tweeting' is about broadcasting daily short burst messages to the world, with the hope that your messages are useful and interesting to someone. Conversely, Twitter is about discovering interesting people online, and following their burst messages for as long as they are interesting.

How Does Twitter Work? - Twitter is very simple to use as broadcaster or receiver. You join with a free account and Twitter name. Then you send broadcasts daily, or even hourly. Go to the 'What's Happening' box, type 140 characters or less, click Tweet and you will most likely include some kind of hyperlink. To receive Twitter feeds, you simply find someone interesting (celebrities included), and 'follow' them to subscribe to their tweet micro blogs. Once a person becomes uninteresting to you, you simply 'un-follow' them. You then choose to read your daily Twitter feeds through any of various Twitter readers.

How Twitter can help your business - Twitter can connect your business to what people are talking about. With over 400 million Tweets a day and over 200 million active users, people turn to Twitter to bring them closer to things they care about, whether it's the news that affects their lives, or the business down the road; why not make it your business?

Use Twitter as a marketing Tool - Thousands of people advertise their businesses or their retail stores by using Twitter, and it does work. The modern internet-savvy user is tired of television advertisement. People today prefer advertising that is faster, less intrusive and can be turned on or off at will...and Twitter is exactly that. Learn the nuances of tweeting and you can get good advertising results by using Twitter.

Be careful when using Twitter as it can be time-consuming if you don't manage it carefully. Customers who would normally not have bothered writing or calling with a complaint or comment may now expect an immediate response when they post a tweet about your business. This may pressure you into trying to respond to every post and not having time to deal with wider issues. You may also find you spend a lot of time reading other people's posts on Twitter and become distracted from your other work.

LinkedIn

LinkedIn is a social networking site designed specifically for the business community. The goal of the site is to allow registered members to establish and document networks of people they know and trust professionally. A LinkedIn member's profile page emphasizes employment history and education. Basic membership for LinkedIn is free. Network members are called "connections." Unlike other free social networking sites like Facebook or Twitter, LinkedIn requires connections to have a pre-existing relationship.

Critical place to find new employees - If you're looking to expand your business and you want to find the best talent, LinkedIn is the perfect channel for you to use. As you may be aware, the best talent is not necessarily looking for work right now as they are already comfortable in their current positions. So a great way to get access to the best talent is by referral via your network.

Browse company profiles - Not only does the 'companies' section act as an additional and very effective marketing tool for your own business, but you can also use it to view real-time information and gather competitive intelligence. This recently updated section provides insights into companies' services and products; current career opportunities; employee insights including current and past employee trends, recommendations, skills and locations.

Networking - Finding vendors, suppliers, manufacturers, and other third party resources is a breeze with LinkedIn. The platform is designed to connect people and companies with like interests, and your chances of finding a partner you can trust are greatly increased with the power of the network. Rather than combing through a phone book and comparison price shopping for days or even weeks before choosing a vendor, you can send a couple of In Mails and be done in just a few hours. In addition, seeing the vendor's online presence gives a more complete picture of a company than just speaking to someone on the phone might, so you can see if other businesses have had good experiences working with the vendor.

Lead Generation - Networking with possible consumers by optimizing your account profile and company page, as well as consistently posting relevant and unique content, are both key elements of getting the most from the social network. A direct result of continuing to build a more coherent and focused brand is the generation of new leads that will come about organically as people find you on LinkedIn and like what they see. This method combines all the best aspects of traditional word-of-mouth lead generation with the control of showing customers your best side by choosing what to include in your profile.

As you continue to use LinkedIn you will experience more and more added benefits for your company.

There are several other Social Media websites that you can utilize. Some of them are:

Pinterest; Google Plus+; Tumblr; Instagram; Vine; Meetup; Ask.fm ... and the list goes on and on.... please use them to your advantage - they are free.

You might say the above-mentioned only applies to social media, but what about the funding for my properties? The strategies in my book apply to born Canadians as well as legal immigrants to Canada. You can start with one condo or a single family home. My strategies in chapter eight teaches you how to finance your property, even with no money down. Like I said, let yourself be known in a community; even if you have to volunteer, go out and make yourself known.

People just want to know that you are honest, you are stable, you work with integrity and you know what you are doing, and they will trust you with their money. Start small and prove yourself, and gradually move up. Be trustworthy, do not be selfish, do not be negative. Help someone get what they want and you will get what you want!

You might be saying "Do you know how negative my culture is?" My answer would be "yes" because I have been there. I have experienced people in my own culture who asked me to show them how real estate investing is done. When I meet with them and show them how I do it, they look at what I am getting out of it and not what they are achieving. In some cases I am making $1,000 and they are making $2,000 plus my knowledge, but they walk away without doing business because they want me to make "0" and themselves to make $3,000 (100%) plus my knowledge. I am not saying that everyone in my culture is like that; all I am saying is, it does exist in my culture, but I just move on to others within my culture who understand business.

When you're not familiar with a culture the default is often to think about a stereotype. You may not even realize that is what you do. For example, many people may think all Americans are loud or all Canadians are in a hurry and say 'eh'. It's first important to realize that you are prejudging someone even if you're not conscious of it. The next step is to stop focusing on where you may be different from that other person, and instead focus on where you might be the same. What do you have in common?

Second, seek help in understanding the culture and the way things are done. In other words, turn any discomfort you may feel into an opportunity to learn and connect. If you spend a little time learning the various cultures, life can be more satisfying. Some of the things that you will learn in different cultures are:

1. When entering a Korean home, you must remove your shoes. To do any less is a sign of great disrespect. Koreans have a special relationship with their floor, on which they sit and often sleep. A dirty floor is intolerable in their homes.

2. Italians - Italians who are friends greet each other with a kiss, usually first on the left cheek, then on the right. When you meet a new person, shake hands.

3. For Chinese - A handshake is the most common form of greeting, or just a nod.

4. Indians do not eat food or pass objects with their left hand. The left hand is considered to be unclean in India as it's used to perform matters associated with going to the bathroom. Therefore, you should avoid your left hand coming into contact with food or any objects that you pass to people.

5. Hugging, kissing or touching - Most Americans prefer a firm handshake as a first greeting. Hugging is reserved for close family members and friends. Kissing people in greeting is a more intimate affair; it's usually done only in the context of relatives, lovers, and friends.

6. Shake hands and introduce yourself when meeting Canadians for the first time. Always shake hands firmly when meeting or departing. Eye contact is important.

7. Academic titles and degrees are important to French Canadians. You should know and use them properly.

8. Initial greetings for Filipinos are formal and follow a set protocol of greeting the eldest or most important person first.

9. British business people always greet by shaking hands. Greetings are somewhat formal. The better your posture the confidence you exude. People should be addressed formally. No hugs, kissing, embracing, touching of the shoulders or elbows. Physical contact should be kept to a minimum.

These are a few of the rules of etiquette that you will observe. Please do a little research if you have an occasion to meet someone, whether for personal or business reasons. I have built my portfolio within my culture and outside of my culture because there are thousands of people from other cultures who can appreciate people for who they are and what they do. I would suggest that if you cannot make it within your culture just move on to another. Some cultures do speak other languages but you will find someone within that culture who speaks your language, and once you connect with that person and do something positive for them, they will recruit others on your behalf.

The opportunities for you to create wealth in Canada as an immigrant are limitless, regardless of your ethnicity, and I am sure the same goes for other countries. I have researched the United States and found the opportunities for legal immigrants are limitless as well. If I can do it, so can you.

Another example is the Honorable Michael Lee Chin, who was born in Jamaica and immigrated to Canada for want of a better life. Where is he now? He is in Toronto, and is known as a business magnate, investor and philanthropist. He made several investments in Canada, including real estate investments, and now he is one of the richest persons in Canada with a net worth of over CAD$2.0 billion, after pledging millions to Royal Ontario Museum, the Rotman School of Management at the University of Toronto, McMaster University and the Joseph Brant Foundation.

Did anyone try to stop him? I'm not sure, but I know he carried on anyway, and stayed the course. I am telling you, the opportunities are here, enough for everyone to partake. Please remember to give something back to someone when you are blessed with an abundance. Here is another example: An immigrant and his son, Isaac Olowolafe Sr. & Jr., were born in Nigeria and immigrated to Ontario, Canada. They now own a real estate brokerage firm and have a property management firm where they currently own and manage over 200+ properties valued over $100,000,000. They are also licensed brokers. It's all about real estate investing.

They are big earners and they give back to the community. They are supporting the African Studies in particular because they believe Africa's history, culture and contributions to the world are often overlooked. They just pledged $25,000 to establish an endowment fund which is matched by an equivalent grant from the Ontario Trust for Student Support, a program of the Ontario Government.

Every culture has immigrants who have made Canada their home, and they are doing quite well. However, there are millions who are fearful and unsure of how to go about investing in a foreign country. Please read this book in its entirety. It will get you started and build your confidence to 7 Figure Retirement.

Have no FEAR, as this is just an acronym for:
    False
    Evidence
    Appearing
    Real

Why not say instead:
    Forget
    Everything negative
    And
    Run to do real estate investing!

It is important to understand the role of culture in the business in which you are operating. Whatever sector you are operating in, cultural differences will have a direct impact on your profitability. Improving your level of knowledge within the culture in which you are doing business can aid in building competencies as well as enabling you to gain a competitive advantage. I therefore suggest that you start your business within your own culture and gradually move on to other cultures as you gain the experience.

Being aware of basic customer needs is an important aspect as this will give the advantage of conveying your message. In simple terms, if you are aware of the customer's cultural background, you will be able to adopt better and more suitable advertising methods.

Body language is another key factor in cultural differences. As different countries have different ways to convey or share their message - for instance in some countries people tend to speak loudly when sharing ideas, whereas in others people speak softly - it is very important to know what your body language should be when interacting with people. Always conduct research to become aware of your target audience since customer demand, decision making, gender views and ideologies greatly vary from culture to culture.

Communication is the key to success for any business, whether you are operating nationally or internationally, whether you are a native or immigrant; but when operating as an immigrant it becomes even more important due to language barriers. Like I said, find someone in that culture who speaks your language and once you do something positive for them they will spread the word.

There are free interpreters and offices that can assist you with your business plan as well as proposal writing, some of which are specific to immigrants. Some of these resources are sponsored and maintained by the federal, provincial or municipal governments while others are sponsored by private individuals. Please use them to your advantage and they will assist you in achieving your 7 Figure Retirement goal. I will set out a few of them below and you may also use my glossary of terms at the back of this book for additional resources.

Bigger Pockets - http://www.biggerpockets.com

Brampton Multicultural Community Centre is a group of diverse professionals dedicated to enhancing newcomer community engagement - http://www.bmcentre.com

Canada Mortgage and Housing Corp. http://www.cmhc-schl.gc.ca

Contact a local legal aid office for help with legal questions. (http://www.lss.bc.ca/legal_aid/legalAidOffices.php)

COSTI Immigrant Services is a community-based multicultural agency providing employment, educational, settlement and social services to all immigrant communities, new Canadians and individuals in need of assistance - languages@costi.org.

Meet Up - http://www.meetup.com

Research & Publication for employment - http://accessalliance.ca/research/publications/making-jobs-work-resources-achieving-employment-security

Statistics Canada - http://www.statcan.gc.ca.start-debut-eng.html
Remember, we are here to assist you if you so desire -
TT&Tpropertiesinc.com and 7FigureRetirement.com

As an immigrant, I wish you the best of success and hope that you
will never stop progressing toward your goals.

Chapter Three
Multiple Tax Benefits

In order to gain the tax savings as a real estate investor, here are some important tips to put you on the right path:

Get Organized

This advice is applicable anywhere, but pertains especially to taxes. It can be hard to hear, but there are no excuses for having a disorganized business. Organization is an essential skill for any business owner, but especially real estate investors.

From keeping detailed records and receipts to managing expenses, staying organized is critical when tax season rolls around. For those investors that have the ability and the time, self-managing the bookkeeping may be a viable option. There are a handful of very good accounting programs out there that can help in this area.

I actually kept my own books for the first two years I was in business, but quickly learned that it made more sense to contract this out to a good bookkeeper. Most investors learn early on that their time is better spent managing the business rather than buried in the tedium of bookkeeping. Either way, it's crucial that you have a system in place to record and archive all aspects of the business.

Easy Said, Easy Done

In theory, getting organized about keeping your receipts sounds easy. But is it? Yes, it can be. Is it really that beneficial? Yes, according to one real estate entrepreneur. This entrepreneur states how she keeps an envelope tucked in the passenger seat of her car for all her food and toll purchases, a box at her home and a special drawer at her office, right next to her desk. She also keeps a file on her computer, and digitally stores receipts from online spending.

"It is all about having an easily accessible place to put them so you use them," she said. Make a simple plan that you can live with, she advises. Once per week you can compile all your receipts.

Collecting receipts for itemization at tax time has shown her how quickly all the little things can add up. "You don't have a grip on your true expenses if you can't add it all up at the end of the year," she further stated. "If you are paying taxes on income that you really didn't make because you haven't deducted your true expenses, then you are sabotaging the longevity of your business."

Alternatively you can go Digital

Maybe stuffing receipt slips into boxes or desk drawers and then drafting spreadsheets to calculate your monthly spending takes time you just don't have on a daily basis. You're always on the go. Well, several companies have products that can help you manage receipts with just a few clicks of your mouse - or camera phone.

Shoeboxed.com has given small business owners and taxpayers an easy and convenient way to stay organized. Just send your receipts, and Shoeboxed will upload them into a personalized online database.

Lemon.com offers a similar service, but in a more simplified format. All its customers need is a smart phone with the ability to take pictures of their receipts. Through the service's mobile application, users upload their own data directly into their accounts for safekeeping. Online shoppers may even have their receipts emailed directly to their Lemon accounts.

Personal finance tools like Intuit's Mint.com and Quicken offer simple solutions for tracking and categorizing your spending to make things easier at tax time. Many small business owners also use QuickBooks accounting software to easily track income and expenses. Many of these tools will export reports or can transfer data directly into software like TurboTax, to make tax time even easier.

Additional Tax Benefits

The tax benefits of real estate investing are attractive, but until recently many investors had difficulty participating in commercial real estate syndications that could fully take advantage of those tax benefits. Now, however, the advent of real estate crowdfunding sites like Realty Mogul has enabled smaller (though still accredited) investors to participate in real estate projects in ways that bring those tax advantages directly to investors.

The tax benefits of direct real estate ownership are substantial and not generally available to investors in real estate investment trusts (REITs), who do not receive all the tax attributes associated with the actual ownership of real estate. Real estate investments made through a limited partnership (LP) or limited liability company (LLC) structure can be more attractive than REITs for several reasons, but at least some of the appeal lies in the inability of REITs to fully take advantage of the various tax shelter benefits available through the LP or LLC structure.

Diversification

Just as most people don't purchase one stock or mutual fund, the prudent investor knows it is important to vary one's real estate investment. Diversification of a real estate portfolio into different properties and geographical areas is critical. There are opportunities to review real estate in select markets whether it be Canada, The United States of America, Europe, where-ever, as long as you do your homework - to take advantage of growing markets.

Security of Direct Ownership and Control

As an investment, real estate provides the greatest amount of ownership and control. You have security of title to a tangible asset, just like your own home. Our clients maintain complete control of their properties with 100% title ownership. You can sell, hold or re-finance your property whenever you wish.

Depreciation

The primary tax feature of equity real estate investing is the role of the depreciation deduction, which has long played a major part in the popularity of real estate direct participation programs involving LPs or LLCs. This is because well-located and well-maintained real property often has a useful life longer than the depreciation recovery periods allowed by law. The depreciation deductions thus effectively create a tax shelter for a property that likely still has a useful life following the investment period. More accurately, the deductions create a tax deferral, since the tax basis of the property is reduced by the amount of the depreciation deductions, increasing the gain (or decreasing the loss) recognized at the time of sale. It should be noted that some or all of this additional gain may be recaptured in the form of ordinary income, as opposed to capital gain.

A particular advantage of the depreciation rules is that the basis for depreciation write-offs is the full cost of the asset. Rarely is real estate purchased for all cash; usually, the major portion of its cost is financed through a mortgage loan or other types of debt financing. The owner, however, gets a full depreciation deduction whether or not he pays all cash for the property, and whether or not he makes any sort of personal guarantee on a financing loan. The reasoning for not limiting the depreciation deduction to an owner's equity stake is that eventually the owner will have to amortize the debt obligation to complete his investment in the property. In practice, however, mortgages usually amortize at a slow pace during the early years of ownership, and many investments are limited to 5-10 year hold periods. Generally, then, even when depreciation deductions are compared with loan repayments, the deductions may generate more current tax savings than the outlays allocated to principal repayment on the loan.

The real kicker is that you can depreciate the cost of residential buildings over 25 years, even while they are increasing in value. Say your rental property - not including the land - cost $200,000. The annual depreciation deduction is $7,300, which means you can have that much in positive cash flow without owing any income taxes. That is a nice benefit, especially if you own several properties. Commercial buildings must be depreciated over a much longer 39-year period, but the depreciation write-offs will still shelter some of your cash flow from taxes.

Loan Interest Deductions

Every year, millions of landlords pay more taxes on their rental income than they have to. Why? Because they fail to take advantage of all the tax deductions available for owners of rental property. Rental real estate provides more tax benefits than almost any other investment. Often, these benefits make the difference between losing money and earning a profit on a rental property.

A further major tax benefit is the deductibility by the real estate operating entity of mortgage interest expense to shelter the current income from that property. Rental properties purchased using mortgage or other financing can have the associated interest expense deducted from the rental income of that property for purposes of calculating the operating entity's taxable income.

Investors in a real estate LP or LLC usually hope that the pass-through entity will have sufficient depreciation, interest expense, and other deductions to shelter the cash flow from the property and keep that distribution of cash non-taxable (or at least tax-deferred). These shelters can permit the entity's partners (or members) to receive a return similar to a tax-exempt bond; only real estate returns have historically been substantially higher.

Investors may ultimately have to have some of this tax benefit "recaptured" upon a sale or other disposition of the property, but in the meantime they have substantially tax-free use of the distributed cash.

Investors also often hope that the LLC will generate excess deductions and thus net operating losses (NOLs) to offset income they have earned from other passive investments. To fully utilize these, investors must take into account the "passive loss rules" (which generally provide that losses generated by an activity characterized as a passive activity can only shelter income from other activities characterized as passive activities, and cannot offset non-passive income) and the "at risk" rules (which generally limit an investor's ability to utilize losses generated by an activity in a given year to the amount for which the investor is considered "at risk" with respect to such activity) in evaluating the current tax savings to be recognized from a real estate investment. If the depreciation deduction, interest expense and other items result in a net loss, such losses are subject to those passive loss rules. Speak with your accountant for further clarification.

Interestingly, you can also write off all the other standard operating expenses that go along with owning a rental property: utilities, insurance, repairs and maintenance, yard care, association fees, and so forth.

When Should I Incorporate My Real Estate Business?

Just because you can incorporate doesn't mean you should, and vice-versa. Weigh the advice of several professionals – a lawyer, an insurance agent, a lender and an accountant. However, be forewarned: they will have different opinions and you will have to sort through that advice to make the decision that's right for you and your business.

Overall, income from passive sources, including rental income, is initially taxed at the highest rate; about 46 per cent depending on the relevant province. This can be reduced to approximately 20 per cent where dividends are paid to shareholders if applicable. Due to the tax-favoured treatment of dividends, these dividends may generate little or no personal income tax, but may be subjected to taxes at the rate of approximately 30 per cent, depending on your income and province of residence. This potentially creates double taxation.

Active income is income from businesses such as developers and rental income in a corporation with more than five full-time employees amongst associated companies. The first $500,000 of taxable income from these businesses is taxed at the low rate of corporate tax (about 16 per cent, depending on your province, although some provincial limits increase at $400,000).

Beyond the general tax rates, a wide assortment of other tax issues will be revealed during your conversations about incorporation with your accountant. The most important thing to remember here is that your situation is unique and demands a unique approach.

Canadians are allowed to deduct interest charges where they use a line of credit, second mortgage, or separate loan to pay for a portion of a property's deposit or various operating expenses related to the property. These expenses can include repairs, utilities and property taxes. The key is being able to trace the payments from the line of credit to the property. Ideally, a separate line of credit is used wholly for investment purposes. Where you require a line of credit for personal use, this should be done with a separate account. This ensures you do not mix amounts spent on your vacation or big-screen TV with those related to your investments.

A variety of financial institutions have debt products which allow you a total amount of debt and then divide this total into multiple accounts you have created. Over time, it may also be possible to restructure your debt so that even otherwise non-deductible interest can be converted into fully deductible interest. To make sure you can take advantage of deductible interest, talk to your tax adviser about what you can do to deduct as much of your interest as possible, and in a method that is acceptable to the CRA.

When you refinance a property you own personally, the interest you paid on the loan may or may not be deductible. It depends on what you used the funds for. If they were used for personal use, the interest is not deductible. On the other hand, if you used the money for qualified investment purposes, the interest will be deductible. The funds received on refinancing will not, however, be taxable.

In a corporation, these mechanics change. Here, if you take funds out of a corporation, they may be taxable regardless of how you use them. Please speak with your accountant.

Grow Your Profit Tax Free

Buying rental property based on speculation of its value is a dangerous tactic since cash flow is the key. However, appreciation over the long run is certainly realistic if you research your location properly. The most valuable is the tax deduction allowed for depreciation of the property. As a result of this it is very common for the investment to generate considerable net income while only half or even less is taxable.

With real estate, you can cash out some of your profits without being taxed. To do so, you simply refinance your property by arranging a new mortgage. Your tax-free profits can then be re-invested, further compounding their growth potential.

Tax deferral

Real estate profits are not taxed until you sell the property. For example, if you purchase a home for $100,000 and it appreciates to $150,000, the $50,000 gain is protected from taxes until you sell it. This allows your investment to grow tax-free year after year, further compounding its growth. This option is to re-mortgage the house or get a line of credit against it to buy another investment property and again, it's tax-free.

Pay no taxes on the cash flow from your property

In addition to equity growth; your real estate investment also generates an income through rental income. You can deduct this income by using the Capital Cost Allowance (CCA), or depreciation rate. As your property appreciates in value, the building's physical wear and tear can be deducted against any income you earn. You pay no taxes on that portion of income until you sell. Get 50% of your profits tax-free (capital gains). From a tax perspective, real estate profits are treated as capital gains. This means only 50% of your capital gains are taxed, unlike interest earnings from bonds and GICs. In other words, 50% of your profits are tax-free.

Tax deduction advantages

Finance and operating costs such as mortgage interest, property management fees, property taxes, repair and maintenance – all of these can be claimed as deductions from your generated growth income.

Let someone else pays for your investment

Your tenants literally pay for your investments. Most income-producing investments properties have this advantage.

Over time, with inflation, your rental income increases, the value of the income producing property investment increases, and your mortgage payments decrease, as the principal is paid off effortlessly. Regardless of what happens in the real estate market, you will own your investments free by clear courtesy of your tenant! Some areas have near 0% vacancy rates; so almost 100% occupancy on your residential investment property.

Tax benefits are unique to each individual investor/buyer. I suggest you speak with an independent accountant to identify what benefits or opportunities apply to your individual situation. You can also contact TT&T Properties Inc. so that we can make an appointment to sit with you and show you our concept of income-producing real estate investment highlights in ownership. You can sell, hold or re-finance your property whenever you wish.

As an immigrant real estate investor, you are entitled to all of the above-mentioned tax benefits.

Chapter Four
Location! Location! Location! - Where To Invest:

In this chapter I will outline my successful process for planning, selecting and acquiring investment properties. You will discover how to complete essential research or due diligence before initiating a purchase, how to arrange the steps involved in closing a deal, how to work with your network of contacts to support your success, and how to strategically manage your portfolio of investments to increase your wealth.

Although the goals for acquiring real estate can vary, I find that careful planning always produces the most success for investors. This planning begins with detailed area research to verify that you will be investing in a region that is economically strong and poised for future growth. It is only after making this determination that you begin the process of selecting and analyzing specific properties.

Economic Fundamentals Not Emotions

Understanding economic fundamentals is an important part of becoming a successful real estate investor. You should have a solid grasp of what is happening in an area where you are planning to invest. Don't get caught up in looking only at past performance. You need to be concerned about what the future holds for that area. Specifically, look for cities or towns that are poised for future growth, with economic development offices actively involved in attracting business into the region.

The amount of information you will have access to may seem overwhelming. However, once you develop a system of information gathering and begin to understand the factors that will impact your investment, you will be able to identify statistics and figures that are useful for determining whether or not to begin investing in that region.

My philosophy has always been to keep it simple.

You can commence with basic information gathering by doing the following:

1. Read the local papers to get a feel for the community.

2. Visit or call the local economic development office and ask how they plan to attract business and people to their city/town.

3. Contact the local planning department to find out what infrastructure improvements are currently taking place or are planned for the future.

4. Do research online, for example, to get a feel for the local housing market on Canadian cities. Visit www.cmhc.ca or www.statistics canada.com for information on demographics. To get information on American cities you can visit www.hud.gov regarding the housing market or www.census.gov for information on demographics.

5. Join a local investment club, a business club or Meet-up to make potentially useful connections or talk with other investors who already invest in that area.

Certain key factors will help you to gather the right information and correctly interpret the results of your research. These include: the basic economics of supply and demand; area demographics and understanding forecasts and trends; determining the cycles of the local real estate market; recognizing an area's political climate and how it will impact your investment; evaluating the infrastructure, both existing and planned and identifying a desirable location.

One thing to remember - real estate is not a race; it is more like a transit system. If a property comes along that's not going to take you towards your destination (your plan of action), let it go by and wait for the one that will.

The Law of Supply and Demand

It is easy to be swayed by what is portrayed in the media. Being able to separate facts from headlines will allow you to make a more informed decision. Rather than focusing on the negative gloom and doom, focus on the trends that are being depicted, and the opportunities that present themselves during these periods.

As with any investment, real estate goes through cycles that are a result of changes in consumer opinion. As an investor, you need to be aware of how this affects the housing market in the areas you invest in. Please be encouraged to understand the basic laws of supply and demand. This way, when you read or listen to economic forecasts and updates you will have a better understanding of the mechanisms behind the changes that are occurring or being predicted.

 Here is a brief summary of these two principles. The law of demand states that there is an inverse relationship between the price of a good and the amount of the good that the buyers will purchase. For example, as prices start rising, other things being constant, consumer demand starts declining.

The law of supply states that there is a direct relationship between the price of good and the amount of the good offered for sale. Therefore, as the price of the product increases, other things being constant, suppliers will attempt to maximize profits by increasing the quantity of the product sold.

Yes, you can make just about any piece of real estate work just as you can make almost any stone skip, but the point is, how much effort does it take to do it? Properties that fit your system feel effortless, just like the perfect skipping rocks. Those that don't fit take a huge amount of your time and energy. Make your real estate investing easy and you'll buy more, reach your goal quicker and have much more fun doing it.

One real estate billionaire stated that economic trends and real estate are tightly linked. "Interest rates are going to go up because employment is going to go up. If employment goes up, then our apartments get filled. If employment goes up, our office buildings get filled. The reality is that increased economic activity combined with increased interest rates is basically bullish for real estate."

The Four Seasons Of A Real Estate Cycle

Real Estate Winter: It is said that the real estate winter is when the real estate values drop or stagnate. The economic fundamentals of the market are all out of whack and the future doesn't look very bright. Some parts of the country, where markets remain inactive, are in a continual real estate winter.

During real estate winter, which can last decades in some areas, astute investors will study, research and educate themselves about real estate opportunities. They will analyze other areas in the country looking for signs of real estate spring. They will work on and perfect their action plan. They will make preparation, financially, for the real estate spring.

Real Estate Spring: When the spring segment of the real estate cycle appears, this is the sign to start buying. During this time you should buy as much as you can. These properties will bring you profits that you will harvest during real estate autumn.

Investor's Actions: During real estate spring you buy quality investment properties that fit your system. You add them to your portfolio, making sure they are well looked after - planted in great soil such as the Property Goldmine town - and then you add some more. Always remember to complete your due diligence.

Real Estate Summer: After several years of real estate spring, the market begins to change to summer. This phase of the real estate cycle is an exciting time for a real estate investor. You will start to see the seeds (properties) you planted in the spring growing into profit centres. By following your Action Plan you will have bought the right property in the right town. You will also notice that the values will have begun to increase and that your tenants have paid down your mortgage. Now you will notice a jump in your net worth with all of the equity you have created.

Investor's Actions: In real estate summer, you have many options. You can sit back and tend your properties, managing them for maximum positive cash flow, cleaning and painting them and getting them ready for the harvest. You can also go through the process of refinancing them - taking some of your cash out now. The equity that you take out today won't have any tax payable on it until you sell the property in the future. Now you can reinvest - in other words, buy the odd new property that fits your system by using the money you've taken from the equity in your other properties when you refinanced. During the years of real estate summer, don't ignore your properties just because they are all running well. Tend them like the valuable crops that they are.

Real Estate Autumn: This is the part of the cycle when real estate investing becomes very enjoyable. During these years, the phase we call real estate autumn, you begin to reap the rewards of all your hard work. You begin to harvest all of the real estate seeds you planted way back in the real estate spring. How? By selling off your properties - one by one.

Investor's Action: In real estate autumn you use a whole new system to begin selling your properties while maximizing profits and minimizing taxes, as you will note from the tax section of this book. During autumn it is important to pay attention to the economic fundamentals.

It is easy to get greedy in real estate, and if you let that emotion enter into your investment decisions it will get you in deep trouble. Never believe your own press clippings. That is why it is critical to commit to the insight; "always leave something on the table for someone else."

Demographics

Demographics are the characteristics of a particular population, such as age, race, gender, income and education. It is important to know the population characteristics within the area you plan to invest in because the types of properties that are in demand and the strategies you employ depend on a population's wants and needs.

A city or town with a mature population will have very different housing needs than one with a younger population because these groups are at different stages in their lives. Within a mature population, you may find that there is a trend toward downsizing and a demand for smaller bungalows that are easy to maintain or condos that cater to an aging population. Their children have most likely left the family home to create families of their own, and retirees may want to spend more time travelling or enjoying hobbies that they didn't have time for while working and raising families. In this case finding a property that requires little maintenance may be of utmost importance.

On the other hand, a younger population can drive growth in single-family homes or be receptive to lease-to-own opportunities in their community. Young couples or families are at a phase in their lives where they are looking to purchase their first homes. They may be having children and expanding their families so they may desire to expand into larger homes.

These are just some examples of the ways you can interpret the changing demographics in a region. Once you take the time to identify and understand the groups within the area you are investing in, you can come to a more educated conclusion. You can also subscribe to newsletters or attend real estate events that can help you to stay on top of upcoming trends. The Canadian Mortgage and Housing Corporation (CMHC) hosts seminars that provide useful information and forecasts for regions as well.

How To Identify Where To Invest

There are 10 major keys that affect real estate value, some of which sound obvious, but others are a little more surprising. Each of these affects real estate prices in both directions, and each one is an important component in finding which way real estate values will be going. You will soon be using media and government announcements as well as watching the news with a whole new set of eyes - eyes trained on finding real estate opportunities.

It is important to picture in your mind a property or region where the event is occurring. This will help plant in your mind the habit of watching for opportunities everywhere you go. Remember, not all towns see real estate values increase in a booming market and many underperform, even in an average market. Our job as millionaire investors is to pick the area that will provide us the best returns for the lowest risk. Bear in mind that you should identify the towns with a future, not a past.

Key No.1: Mortgage Interest Rates - these rates are discussed in the media just about every day, yet even though they have become a national obsession, many people don't understand how interest rates work. The most obvious assumption is that low mortgage rates drive values upward, while high interest rates keep values down. Using this theory, you would think that a low interest rate environment is good for real estate investor. However, this assumption is false. Sure, a low mortgage interest rate keeps the investor's expenses down but it also allows more renters to become home owners, thus increasing vacancy rates. So, record low interest rates are actually more of a neutral issue for investors.

Key No.2: Net Wealth Effect, Increase in disposable incomes - This factor is often overlooked, or discounted by investors, but it's one of the most important numbers to track as an indicator of future value. If a town's average disposable income is increasing faster than the provincial average, real estate prices are poised to do the same. Here are the key indicators of the New Wealth Effect (remember you must compare the region's numbers vs. the provincial and national averages: (a) Increased Average Income (b) Decreasing Income Tax Rates and (c) Increasing Retail Sales. You can use statscan.gc.ca website for up-to-date information.

Key No.3: Increased Job Growth and Intra-Migration: A major increase in demand, without a corresponding increase in supply, will always drive prices upwards. However, in the real estate market it is important to know the reasons behind the increase in demand, so you can be assured that the increase is being driven by fundamentals, not speculation.

When analyzing this component, you are looking for cities, towns and neighbourhoods in high demand because of an increase in jobs or easier access to jobs. Always be on the lookout for major announcements of new jobs, major expansions or new employers moving into an area. You want to find areas where the population is growing faster than the provincial average and are gaining a reputation as a great place to live.

Analyze both components of in-migration:
(1) Immigration - people moving from other countries to Canada.
(2) Intra-migration - people moving from other parts of Canada into the area.

Key No.4: The Real Estate Doppler Effect - With this fundamental, you will find that it is often much more profitable to surround the boom than invest right in the heart of it. To picture the Real Estate Doppler Effect, imagine you are standing at the side of a pond holding a large stone. Now throw this stone out as far as you can into the pond. There is an initial splash where the stone hits the water. Then, in a perfect circle around this initial splash, a large ripple flows outwards. Subsequently, outside of that ripple another ripple forms, this time a little smaller.

This phenomenon occurs exactly the same way in the real estate market. When a specific area has a boom in prices, the real estate in the surrounding areas follows, but often not at the same rate as the initial splash area. You can use this factor to identify areas that are poised for a strong increase in values.

On the macro scale, for example, when a larger city has a boom, property values in areas surrounding it get pushed upwards in the following months and years.

This also works on a micro scale. When a neighbourhood is redeveloped or goes through gentrification, the older untouched neighbourhoods near it also increase in value. A specific investment strategy is to look for these redeveloping areas and then purchase in areas surrounding them where it is still possible to find good properties at great prices, before the positive boom hits the region.

Key No.5: Political Climate - As a real estate investor, you must keep your eyes and ears open to the shifts in political winds. What you are looking for is a business-friendly environment with minimal taxation (both income and property) and with a fair Landlord and Tenant law structure. In a perfect world, you are looking for an area with strong growth in both new industries and new jobs so that there are more potential renters. As a real estate investor, it is important to understand that you are in business (even if you only own one property) and anything that enhances your business's ability for success should be applauded and supported.

Business Friendly Generally Equals Real Estate Friendly - Jobs and taxation directly affect real estate values - look for regions where development is wanted, not shunned. Real estate investment is a complicated business impacted by the local Economic Development office. In a perfect investment world, you will find an area with the potential to attract and sustain a good supply of quality renters and eventual buyers. That means an area with strong economic growth potential in terms of new industries and new jobs. It also means finding a business-friendly environment with minimal taxation (personal and property) and with a fair landlord and tenant law structure! If you find a region with a dynamic and forward looking Economic Development office, you have just identified an area that has a great potential for attracting employers.

At the same time, watch out for critical infrastructure expansion. This is another instance where reading major and local newspapers every day can pay off. You will see opportunities everywhere! Paying attention will pay you dividends.

Key No.6: Areas of Gentrification and Renewal - Areas of renewal provide tremendous opportunity for a sophisticated investor. They often, if chosen correctly, have consistently proven to provide the biggest bang for your investment dollars. Renewal areas are best defined as neighbourhoods that are moving up from one economic class to the next. These tend to be older areas that are rediscovered and redeveloped. Often these areas will be described as "tough yet funky," meaning the neighbourhood has character and with a little cleaning up will prove to be an amazing place to bring up a family.

You will identify these neighbourhoods quite easily. In renewal areas you will witness a mixture of old run-down homes that have a lot of character and houses that have recently been fixed up, along with new homes being built where older ones were torn down (in-fills). You will also witness older abandoned warehouses being converted to coveted loft apartments. Pride of ownership will be starting to shine through.

KEY INSIGHT
LOOK FOR RENEWAL AREAS WHICH ARE LOCATED NEAR AREAS THAT HAVE ALREADY GONE THROUGH THE GENTRIFICATION PROCESS. THAT WAY, NOT ONLY WILL THE REGION BE AFFECTED BY ITS OWN RENEWAL, BUT WILL ALSO BE AFFECTED BY THE REAL ESTATE DOPPLER EFFECT. NEVER BE THE FIRST INTO AN AREA YOU BELIEVE IS GOING TO BE IN TRANSITION. RENEWAL AREAS HAVE LOTS OF LONG-TERM PROFIT POTENTIAL.

Key No. 7: Maximizing Value And Zoning Opportunities - Always look for ways to make a good deal better, making sure the property is performing at its highest and best use.

Sophisticated investors learn to first look at a property's physical attributes, where the property is located and what it's used for. Then they examine how they may be able to change that property's use to optimize profit, an investment strategy that goes way beyond renovating and existing property to add re-sale value.

For example, you could purchase an old run-down hotel and convert it to condominiums or rental units. This takes the property from a below average performer to its highest and best use, a cash flow and value winner. The same can be true if you are buying raw land and selling it off by the building lot, thus increasing the overall value of the property.

Another example involves buying a property that is currently a single family dwelling and converting it to a multi-family or student housing property. You will need to know your local zoning and tenant regulations to make this transition successful; however, these simple changes will dramatically affect not only the value of the property but the income you generate from it.

"Highest and best use" is the term you will see in many professional property appraisals. This details what the property would be used for if it was being used to its zoning potential. Your opportunities lie in finding properties that are not being maximized and then changing their use.

Key No.8: Buy Wholesale; Sell Retail - You can buy property wholesale any day of the week, in any town across the country; you just have to know what to look for. There are companies whose sole business is buying properties at wholesale and selling them to investors or homeowners at retail. This are of real estate investing can be very profitable if you know what you are doing.

One example of how it works is - you purchase a larger multi-family property, an entire apartment building. You then convert the property so that each suite has an individual title. This is known as condominiumization or stratification. Now you can sell the individual units one at a time for substantially more than you paid for them.

Another way to buy "wholesale" is to buy properties that are in or about to go into foreclosure. This is where you buy properties from lenders who have foreclosed on unpaid debt or from homeowners trying to avoid bankruptcy or increase their cash flow fast. NEVER, EVER be a vulture and try to steal their property from them for next to nothing just because they are desperate.

Key No. 9: Stand Out From The Crowd - Quality marketing is a critical tool for real estate investors. You need to become proficient at it if you wish to get higher than market rents and values for your properties. By using proven marketing strategies, you can attract the type of buyer, seller or renter you want, while at the same time reducing the effort it takes for you to run your business. Quality marketing is a real estate investor's best-kept secret. It allows you to maximize your income, minimize your purchase price and maximize your selling price.

For instance, if there are two similar houses in the same neighbourhood, the one that is properly marketed can easily sell for 5 percent to 10 percent more than the other. When you are talking real estate, 5 to 10 percent is a lot of money. The same is true for rental properties; simple marketing strategies can allow you to get a higher rent (if your local Landlord and Tenant laws allow) than you would for the exact same property that is poorly marketed. That's how valuable quality marketing is. The good news is, you don't have to be overly creative to be a good marketer. Marketing is not an art; it is a science with proven formulas that you can follow to be successful. Stick to the chapters of this book and you will be successful.

KEY INSIGHT
MATCHING YOUR MESSAGE TO YOUR PROSPECTIVE TARGET IS CRITICAL. IF YOU ARE TRYING TO GET A MORTGAGE, TARGET YOUR MESSAGE AND PRESENTATION TO A BANKER'S POINT OF VIEW. IF YOU ARE TRYING TO ATTRACT MOTIVATED SELLERS FOR YOUR PROPERTY, MAKE SURE YOU ARE SPEAKING THEIR LANGUAGE. IN OTHER WORDS, PUT YOURSELF IN THEIR SHOES, THINK ABOUT WHAT THEY WILL BE LOOKING FOR - THEN GIVE IT TO THEM WHEREVER POSSIBLE.

Key No.10: Renovations And Sweat Equity - Doing renovations on a property can dramatically affect its value. Many investors start this way because they don't have a lot of working capital but they do have time and expertise.

Areas of transition are a great source of properties that need improvements. Look for well-built but somewhat neglected properties in areas that are showing an increase in pride of ownership. The first step is to buy a property in a location that is poised to boom. Make sure the property is structurally sound and just needs simple things like lumber, new flooring, drywall, paint, cabinets and so on. You buy it, improve it to increase the value and the curb appeal and then either sell it or rent it, making it a part of your investment portfolio. The key is, if the property is going to be a rental or if you are just going to sell it, keep the work simple.

Whatever you do, please do NOT be a speculator - do not let your emotions get the best of you. Aim for facts, not rumours. For example, you might hear your neighbour, who knows someone whose brother works on a planning committee somewhere, tells you and all of his friends about a new development or golf course that's about to be built. He says you should go up there and buy property because he heard it's a sure thing. In this situation, people start buying based on greed and this emotional behaviour drives up the value. These speculators forget about economic fundamentals and neglect doing their homework, once again proving that emotions lead to bad decisions and are the downfall of most real estate investors.

Although there might be money to be made in speculation, it is not the right thing to do; there are too many variables that are out of your control.

As an immigrant real estate investor, this is the successful system that I have used is selecting my investment locations. I suggest you follow this system for success.

Chapter Five
Due Diligence

The two resources of a real estate investor are positive cash flow and time. A property will give you positive cash flow if, at the end of the month, the rent you take in exceeds the expenses of operating and owning the property. These expenses include any item you, not your tenant, pay for during the month. Such expenses can include utilities, maintenance, management and insurance, and they always include mortgage and tax payments. You deduct these from the rent you have collected and if you end up with a positive balance, you have a positive cash flow. However, if you come up with a negative balance, this is not good news and you need to fix the situation immediately.

The other important resource is time. Your time is valuable and it would be literally impossible to look at and analyze every single property that comes on the market. You want to focus your time only on properties that have the potential of creating positive cash flow. The Property Analysis Evaluator does just that. It will save you, your realtors and vendors a lot of time. It allows you to have a life outside of real estate, even in real estate spring when you will be buying like crazy.

The 10 Percent Rule: Due to the fact that time is so important, the first level to build on our evaluator is a filter; a way to discard the majority of properties quickly and effectively. This filter is a simple yet power mathematical formula that has been developed from the results of much larger and more complex analysis tool.

The complex formula took lots of time to work through and it had many components such as interest rate, expense ratio, property price, down payment, market demand and other factors. Then one day while analyzing the results of all of these calculations, a very clear mathematical pattern became obvious. Every time a property worked under this formula, there was a direct correlation between the amount of rent it generated and the purchase price. So rather than completing a complex, detailed analysis upfront on every property, you can now use the following formula as your first filter, which gets you closer to achieving your 7 Figure Retirement.

The annual gross rent must be at least 10 percent of the purchase price. If the annual gross rent is 10 percent or more of the purchase price, the property is worth further investigation and a more detailed analysis. If the gross rent is below 10 percent of the purchase price, or the property doesn't have the potential to drive the rent to that level, walk away and keep looking for a better property.

Example of the 10 percent rule calculation

Monthly Rent x 12 = Gross Annual Rent
Purchase Price x 10% must equal Gross Annual Rent or less, therefore:

A property rents for $925.00 per month and you can buy it for $100,000. Does this property warrant more of your valuable time?

$925.00 x 12 = $11,100
$100,000 x 10% = $10,000
The math shows that this property does warrant more investigation. By following this quick math, you can see that the rent far surpasses the 10 percent mark and the property is worth more detailed analysis.

Sophisticated Investor Calculator Step Sample

Purchase Price = $125,000 Monthly Rent =$1,100
_____x 12 =_____
_____x 10% = _____

Is this property worth more of your time: Yes or No?

Once the property fits the 10% rule, you can feel comfortable spending time analyzing it. The first step is to determine the vendor's level of motivation; the more motivated the vendor is, the more likely you will get a better bargain. To find out the level of motivation you can ask the following questions:

1. Why are you selling? (Many vendors have a pre-determined answer. This often requires a follow-up such as "Tell me more...")
2. How long have you owned the property? (This question is designed to determine if the vendors like to flip properties.)
3. When do you have to move? (You will discover if the vendor has a deadline; if so, you'll know their main motivation.)
4. Can I/my client see it tomorrow at .....? (If they are motivated they will jump at the chance to show the property at any time of the day or night. If not you will be brushed off.)

Then comes the power of the Due Diligence Checklist - You start by using the 10 percent rule to narrow down the massive list of for-sale properties to a manageable size. Then you shrink this list even further by focusing only on motivated vendors; still none of this has taken very much of your time. Now you are left with a solid list of properties that have potential, then you are ready to dive into the details of the property itself.

Here is a checklist of questions that you need to answer for every property you are analyzing. You will see it is a fairly extensive list. This is your due diligence check list, so make sure every question is answered. If the vendors hesitate to provide answers to some questions, consider it a signal and dig a little deeper to find out why. Are they hiding something that might be important to you?

Completing this checklist fully is another piece of that extra 10 percent of effort that many are not willing to take on. Your job is to collect all of this information in one place and look for any inconsistencies in the answers.

As you use this checklist, you will discover that it forces you to look at the fundamentals behind the property, further removing your emotions from your decision. You will also hone your instinct for identifying quality properties by having these conversations with the vendors or realtors. At the beginning it may feel like a lot of extra work; however, the more practice you get, the quicker and more efficient you will become. The more efficient you become the more successful your investments will be. The more successful your investments, the closer you are to achieving your 7 Figure Retirement.

Each property should have its own Due Diligence Checklist - Due diligence is critical for ANY property you are considering investing in. Whether you are a silent partner or the actual person finding and investigating a property, you must do your own due diligence. This checklist will provide you a foundation from which to work and will assist you in asking the critical questions:

Location:
- What is the nature of the local economy? Diverse or one major employer?
- Demonstrated economic growth over the last few years?
- In what area of town is the property located? Older....newer....Transitional......?
- What is the type and quality of the surrounding properties?
- Strong and specific growth plan in place to attract businesses to the region and accommodate future expansion?
- Demographics reflecting a young population; population growth that is surpassing the national average; high rate of immigration?
- A region where the median income is higher than the national average?
- Low unemployment rate?
- Forecast of what will be in demand over the next few years in that area based on demographics, sales trends, etc.?
- Historical housing prices and past cycles, vacancy rates and the percentage of housing that is owner-occupied vs. rental dwelling?
- What kind of restrictions are in place for the types of investments you are looking into? (For example, many areas have restrictions or limitations with regard to student rentals)
- Plans for major transportation improvements and infrastructure such as new roads and bridges that will allow easier access into and

within the area? (Look at projected infrastructure change as well as what is currently happening.)
- What is the community's proximity to airports, train stations, highways and other transportation?
- Are there adequate schools, universities, colleges, and plans for future growth?
- Are there available health care facilities?

Building:
- What is the overall curb appeal? (scale 1 to 10)
- What is the overall interior appeal? (scale 1 to 10)
- How well has the property been maintained? (scale 1 to 10)
- Are there any deferred maintenance repairs required in the next 12 months? If YES, list them: List estimated cost of repairs $.....
- Are there any appliances you need to purchase?
- Has a complete professional inspection been completed? If no, when are you scheduling it for?
- Is a Real Property Report (site survey certificate) available from vendor? If YES, is it acceptable to your lawyer for closing?

Additional Due Diligence - Check the following items to ensure you are not buying unknown trouble:
- Confirm taxes and other charges are current (city hall)
- Confirm no outstanding work orders or compliance orders (city hall/health department)
- Who will be managing the property?
- What banker/broker has a program to assist you with the financing on this property?
- What is the vendor's REAL motivation level? (0=none, 10=extremely)
- Do you plan on keeping the current tenant(s)?

Once your due diligence has identified an area or community with solid economic fundamentals, you will be ready to evaluate specific properties. This evaluation will be the main step involved in acquiring the kind of real estate that promises a profitable return on your investment.

Chapter Six
Building Your Power Team

Successful real estate investors and business owners have one thing in common: they always have a team of experts at their disposal. Creating a 'power team' is vital to your wealth building strategy, and you will certainly be lost without experts to advise and guide you on your entrepreneurial journey. Your allies will protect you from financial harm, speed up your wealth creation and help you attain your goals whilst avoiding obstacles along the way.

Real estate is similar to any other business - initially, you will be faced with specialized vocabulary that you have to understand and used effectively. It is not unusual that you might feel awkward working with these unfamiliar terms; however, with time and experience they will become a natural part of your vocabulary. Depending on when you come across these terms or phrases you might be able to self-interpret, but if you do not understand you can make notes and look them up later or alternatively you can ask a trusted source.

Please remember that your success is largely dependent on who you surround yourself with. To become a successful real estate investor, I suggest that you seek relationship/affiliation with other experienced investors and utilize these sources to identify the opportunities that will assist you to develop your portfolio to profitability. It is often said that you become the average of the people you associate with; therefore, you should seek positive, encouraging, inspiring professionals who will motivate you and celebrate your successes.

Here is a list of people that I recommend for your power team. Surely you may add more to this list as you see fit and this list is not in any particular order:

Realtors

A Realtor is of utmost importance in your real estate investment business; however, you need to know their specialty. Do not use a residential realtor to do a commercial deal unless they are trained in the commercial field. I got caught in this scenario as you have read on my Introduction page. Be cautious!

Generally, realtors play a very important part on the team because they have a wealth of information for the business. They are in the field for long hours per day (whether inside or outside) and they continue to perfect their skills to identify good investments for their clients. Some are more experienced than others, while some are more diplomatic than others and some have more patience than others. It is good to start out with several realtors and as you get more seasoned you will realize which ones are understanding of your needs and appreciate your interest. It's all about the realtor finding the right property in the right area and at the right price to enrich your portfolio.

Your realtors will be able to do the area comparables for you so that you can make a more educated decision. They will be able to supply you with specific details such as house type, building type, unit size, location and sometimes market analysis. It is expected that you will tap into all the resources that they have available to assist you to come up with a good calculated decision.

A good realtor will dig deep into what your strategies are, help you to achieve your goal at a faster and safer pace. If your strategy is to buy and hold, the realtor will assist you with detailed expense calculation to determine if there will be positive cash flow. At the end of the day, it's all about buying or walking away!

An experienced realtor will utilize their negotiation skills so that you can get a more favourable price on the property. At times the experienced realtor will introduce creative financing to the vendor. One example is the vendor take back (VTB), a clause which allows the vendor (seller) to hold a second mortgage on the property. In this instance, it will save the vendor (seller) capital gains tax on the portion that is held back and at the same time the purchaser (buyer) will repay that loan at a lower rate than the market value. This is a win-win for both parties.

I would recommend that you choose a realtor who is experienced in the field. You need someone who will make sure all the steps are done correctly from negotiating, making the offer to closing the deal.

The Lawyer

For most people, buying a home is the largest and most significant purchase they'll ever make. Whether you are buying or selling, hiring a real estate attorney early in the process will protect you against the unexpected, and ensure a smooth and low-stress closing.

A real estate lawyer will protect your rights and interests in the transaction…they are the only party truly "on your side." The lawyer has the experience and training to handle the unique issues regarding the property and the problems most people cannot anticipate. They see a lot of contracts and know the local customs and can help cut through roadblocks.

Your lawyer will review the purchase agreement. Suppose there's an illegal structure on the property, or termites, radon, lead paint, asbestos, or other potentially hazardous waste? Inspection contingencies need to be clearly defined. At this point in the process, if you back out of the deal, what happens to your deposit?

Your attorney works with your mortgage loan officer, the other party's attorney and agents to make sure that dates are set for attorney approval, home inspection, title search, mortgage commitment and other contingencies.

Your attorney will also review important documents, including legal descriptions, mortgage loan documents, the property survey, and the title and the title insurance policy. Your attorney will review the deed, to ensure there are no errors in the legal description. Even simple mistakes – a name misspelled, for example – can create big title issues. Make sure you hire a lawyer with years of real estate experience, one who is familiar with things like tax sales, VTB, and cash back on closing. Your lawyer attends the closing, to ensure the process moves along efficiently and effectively. In the case of problems/issues, the lawyer will counsel and represent you. Your lawyer has no direct emotional involvement in the transaction, and no conflict of interest. You'll appreciate an experienced lawyer by your side, if the situation becomes difficult you will have peace of mind! Best to get a referral.

The Mortgage Broker

Mortgage brokers work with multiple lenders, so they have more flexibility in matching a lender to a borrower's situation and needs. Whether it's a less than stellar credit score or a down payment issue, having multiple loan sources is a plus.

When you're talking to mortgage brokers, ask about the lenders they work with. Also make sure they work with all types of loans, including RRSPs. If you ask the average real estate professional what is most likely to delay a closing, most will say that it's the mortgage process. While the mortgage broker may be at the mercy of their underwriters in some respects, they should be all over every deadline and moving documents efficiently to avoid as many problems as possible.

For long-term rental property investing, the investor will need mortgages. Your mortgage broker should be familiar with the special needs of real estate investors, and should be out working their underwriters for financing your deals when the numbers show they're good investments. No matter what your real estate investing niche, flipping to an investor getting a mortgage, holding a property for rental, or some other strategy, if a mortgage is necessary, the mortgage broker is a key player.

The Accountant

Successful real estate investors are those who do the essential things right. For instance, business structuring, tax preparation and deductions management are vital aspects of the real estate business that must be handled scrupulously. It is on these vital things that smart investors outdo the rest of the competition by enlisting the services of professional real estate accountants.

While many new investors wish away the idea of hiring an experienced real estate accountant, smart investors know that having accounting experts saves them lots of money in their investment pursuits.

It is essential to have an experienced real estate accountant as they will structure your operation and investment in a tax efficient manner.

The Inspector

A qualified home inspector combs a property's visible and accessible areas to identify any health and safety problems, positive or negative conditions of the property and any conditions that need further specialized attention.

An inspection includes structural elements such as the roof, foundation, walls, windows, doors, insulation, basement or crawlspace and attic. Electrical, plumbing, heating and cooling systems are also part of a home inspection. It can even include examination of appliances and should also report any evidence of termites.

Once the inspection is complete, a home inspector provides a written, comprehensive report detailing any issues with the home and in most cases there are photographs attached.

Some important things to remember about home inspection reports: No home is perfect. It is not uncommon for a report to include 50 or more issues. This is not "pass" or "fail." The inspection gives you the information you need to decide whether or not to buy the home "as is" or negotiate with the seller to either fix (some of) the problems or reduce the price.

This is not a warranty. The report identifies issues found the day of inspection and cannot predict problems that may arise a few months or a few days down the road. It is recommended that an inspector is hired as they will ensure that your property is in good condition.

It's a good idea to accompany your home inspector so you can ask questions and see the good and not-so-good for yourself.

The Contractor

A general contractor oversees and manages large home improvement and remodeling projects, acting as your main contact and ensuring the work is done to your satisfaction. While it's not unreasonable to think that a real estate investor could act as their own general contractor (and save on the expense), it's a difficult role that requires real skill, expert knowledge and lots of time on-site. Before you choose a contractor, here are some steps that you may take in order to make the job less stressful:

Step No.1 - Educate yourself. It's important to educate yourself about the work you want to have completed prior to meeting with contractors. This way, you'll have a deeper understanding of renovation lingo, you'll be able to provide the contractor with enough information to prepare an estimate that meets your goals, be able to interpret any estimates that you receive, and to figure out whether the contractor is overpricing their work.

Step No. 2 - Check contractor references and past experience. To select the best of the best, you will need to check company's procedures, specifications, references and the way they communicate with you. If the construction company or contractor does not know how to communicate well with you (even when the others have no problems), the possibility for misunderstandings in the project increases, and that means higher costs and less satisfaction.

Step No. 3 - Read contractor reviews. Look for contractors affiliated with the Better Business Bureau, National Association of the Remodeling Industry (NARI), National Kitchen and Bath Association (NKBA), National Association of Home Builders (NAHB) or any other local building or association. Look at each Contractors website to see what type of work they perform, any examples of already completed work and their qualifications.

Step No. 4 - Make a list of questions that the contractor must answer. When you look at the specifications of potential contractors, make a list of questions which you want to be answered. Those who respond to your e-mail or call you should have an advantage over the others. Nevertheless, consider whether your questions were answered clearly. This is particularly important for issues that you are not clear about or you did not understand.

Here are some questions you need to ask each contractor:

Did the contractor omit a portion of the scope of work? If so, have them revise the estimate. Are they using lesser quality materials (paint, cabinets, tile, etc.)? How long will it take to complete the work? Are they insured with a General Liability policy? Can they provide a minimum of 3 to 5 references from previous projects? Are permits necessary and if so, is the cost included in the estimate? Is the contractor willing to let you visit several of their jobs? What type of warranty does the contractor provide? If they do not understand what you are talking about, ask more questions. Good builders are the ones who know how to solve a problem. However, those who insist on answering your questions and want to explain you every little detail are the best.

Step No. 5 - Show the contractor what you want completed. During your meetings, hand over your information that you compiled and walk the job with each of them. Be prepared to answer numerous questions. Some will be easy to answer and others may need some additional research on your part. Either way, try to stick with your initial scope of work and do not deviate because it will only make it more difficult for you to interpret the figures on each bid. Ask each contractor how long it will take them to prepare the estimate and make sure they honour those dates. If they don't, that should be a red flag.

Step. No. 6 - The cheapest offers are often the most expensive. Price should not be the deciding factor when choosing contractors. People often choose the lowest bid and ultimately discover that the contractor has not done the job properly. High quality papers require a certain price. It may cost you more, but the job will be done smoothly and within the standards of eligibility. Cheaper can offer more chop at the end, because you'll eventually change the order, to correct errors or the contractor to cancel the job. If you ask for three bids for your project, you'll get three different prices. If a contractor is 15 percent more expensive than another, ask him why. Maybe it includes more items in his offer. If it is cheaper by 15 percent, maybe he forgot to include something very important to you. Remember, you have the right to ask a contractor what you want and they must know how to explain the offer.

A good experienced contractor with years of experience can also recognize and advise you on potential dangers or problems with the property.

The Insurance Agent

Whether the insurance agent is working for an insurance agency or brokerage, an insurance carrier or independently, insurance agents help businesses and individuals select insurance products that provide the financial protection they need.   I am suggesting that you hire an experienced, astute insurance agent who will arrange for reasonable insurance premiums on your investment properties, ones that will best suit your needs.

Ability and Flexibility – When you are looking for an insurance agent, one of the most frustrating things in the world can be getting stuck with an agent whose doors are open at 8 a.m. and close at 4 p.m. Ask your potential insurance agent what kind of schedule they normally work, in case you need to be able to get hold of them. Determine whether their company has a 24-hour help line or if you will have to wait for the next business day to get help.

It is important for you to hire insurance agents who are familiar with your line of business. The more familiar they are to your line of business the more advantageous it will be to you and your business. You may also seek referrals.

The Appraiser

An appraiser will walk through the property outdoors and go through from room to room to determine its condition. He/she will note any amenities. With a camera in hand and a sketch book and pencil, the appraiser will record the layout of the property assessment. If he/she notices any health violations or compromised safety codes he will request that they be fixed before the property is sold. Until they are fixed the purchaser could have problems getting the loan approved by the lender.

An experienced appraiser will have an accurate assessment of the value of the different investments, such as commercial and residential buildings and land. Their worth to you lies in their ability to determine the fair market value of your prospective investment, backing up their conclusions with factual information and a competent knowledge of the three most common methods that appraisers use. These methods are:

1. Direct or replacement cost method - This is estimating the current cost to reconstruct the property, including all improvements at the date of the appraisal, less depreciation. The value of the land is then added to this figure.
2. Direct sales comparison method - This is the most commonly used method. The appraiser would look at recent sales of properties of similar size, quality and location to determine the market value of the property he analyzed. Assuming that the price paid for recent sales is indicative of what buyers are willing to pay and is a good reflection of fair market value.

3. Income capitalization method - This is generally used for properties that generate income. The present value is directly related to its net operating income or projected net operation income.

It is advantageous for the sophisticated investor to understand the various methods and fundamentals behind the valuation of property in order to stay informed and educated so that he/she can make solid investment decisions. This is also helpful when you are entering a new region as it will allow you to calculate locate market values.

Advise on Mortgage Financing - Prior to waiving the subject to financing condition on your offer, be sure to have a mortgage commitment letter from your mortgage lender. A verbal approval on your mortgage application should never be an option as this is not a legal commitment. Do not remove your mortgage financing condition without a written approval confirmation. In the event that this should occur it could cause a delay in the application process; however, you can write a letter of explanation to the seller and in most cases it will be accepted.

Closing the Deal - The closing date is set during negotiation of the Agreement of Purchase and Sale. It is usually many weeks or months after the purchaser's offer is formally accepted by the vendor. If it is residential property the period is usually shorter than that of a commercial property. In most cases the commercial property has to go through additional inspection than a residential property, including environmental assessment.

Prior to the closing day both vendor and purchaser can experience a time of emotion and/or excitement. Closing on a property means that all conditions have been met and therefore waived. Once these conditions are waived, including the sales contract and loan agreement, both the vendor and purchaser are obligated to complete the transaction. If the purchaser fails to close the deal it could cause the deposit to be forfeited and/or a possibility of a lawsuit.

At the point of closing, the lawyer has searched title and found it to be in good standing, the mortgage funds are ready to be disbursed and the paperwork on the purchase is ready to be signed and recorded. At the successful end of this transaction, the deed and mortgage are recorded and the transaction is closed. This is the time (in most cases) when the property is now turned over to the purchaser.

The aforementioned will be the main focus of your power team. Once again, as an immigrant in this country, this is the team that I work with and this is how I select them. It works well for me so this is my recommendation for you, in selecting your power team.

Chapter Seven
Execute Your Plan of Action – Build Your Portfolio

Now that you have got to this chapter of my book, it is time to take action. Now what????

If you are new to real estate investing, use this book as your guide to get the background information that you need to get started. Use it to develop a thorough understanding of the basics, keep implementing them and keep the energy active. Remember, whatever is hard is good. It might seem hard in the beginning but once you find the niche that you enjoy, it becomes more easy and rewarding each time you close on a deal.

If you need help you can reach out to us at anytime and we will be there to assist - 7figureretirement.com or tt&tpropertiesinc.com. You can also bookmark this book; it belongs to you, so use it as your guide. Remember to surround yourself with like-minded people. Join a real estate investment group or a business group - one that will keep you motivated. Define your end goal, where you want real estate investing to take you, how much you need to achieve it, and don't stop until you get there; it's not hard if you put your heart in it!!

Still having doubts, wondering about your bad credit score? If your answer is yes that should not prevent you from taking action. Remember there are several ways to start building wealth with real estate. While you are waiting to have an acceptable credit score for the bank, prove yourself to others and use other people's money (OPM) to build your portfolio. The fact that your credit score is lower than the bank requires should not prevent you. Revisit chapter 8 and see the many ways in which you can purchase properties even with low credit scores. Remember, this is your guide; it must be utilized effectively to obtain favourable results.

What else is bothering you? No money for the down payment? There are many real estate millionaires who achieved wealth without using any of their own money. If I knew how they did it years ago I would have written this book years ago. I learnt it recently, hence my book is just written and you can find the answer right here. Please release yourself of all the doubt, fears, intimidation, nervousness, etc. etc. and use this book as your armour for success. Try using a "vision board." Cut out pictures of the things you desire and the goals you wish to achieve, and place the board where you will see it most often so that you can be reminded of your destination. It's your time to be successful; go for it!

Fearful of losing money? Most millionaires will tell you that they lost money while making money. The Bible tells you that a just man falls seven times, and rises up again. Ask Donald Trump how much he has lost and ask him how rich he is today. Remember in my introduction I explained how much I lost in my first deal, but I did not stop there. I used it as a learning tool and kept moving forward. Do not allow fear to get the better of you. It will cripple you; it will diminish your positive mindset. Most winners have failed at least once in their life but they are smart enough to use the negative experience as a stepping stone to advance further. Indulge yourself in positive thinking; for example, look at the glass half full rather than half empty. Just decide to step out of your comfort zone, tell yourself that you were not created with a spirit of fear but of love, power and sound mind, and fear will go; you are bigger than fear. Achievement is yours; claim it!

Oh Yes! I know what else is keeping you back - Those things that kept a lot of us back when we first started. Those so called friends or is it family members who are telling you that it is impossible? Let that statement motivate you and show them that it can be done. It will be done in record time also because you are using this guide and instead of spending years being that real estate speculator you will immediately become that real estate sophisticated investor. My advice to you is, if anyone is keeping you back with the negativities just purge them from your call list or your socializing list and revisit them in two years when you have attained your goal. At this time, guess what? They will now want to be your friend because they will want to know how you did it. Just say "Buy that book, *7 Figure Retirement* - the author is Lurline Henriques." Factor your mindset for success!

Would you like some more help? Here we go...

You can start by setting your goals. It is absolutely critical to not lose your momentum. Once you set your goals stay on track, be positive, stay focused. For each goal you set and achieve, the next one must be bigger.

Think of yourself as a house. The first place that you build is the foundation. Without the foundation you will have no house, and if the foundation is not solid the house will not last long. Therefore you need to build a solid foundation. How do you build a solid foundation, you might ask? The first thing you will do is proper planning. You can plan by yourself or you can plan with someone who you trust. Someone who will understand your vision and can brainstorm with you. However you decide to do it, please document everything.

Keep your "WHY" in check. Always think of why you are doing real estate investing, where you want it to take you, what kind of properties you expect to own and the timeline to accomplish all of this. Think long term - do not think of the journey - no one said it is a straight line; it might not be, but think of the destination. Where you want to be and how long it should take you to get there. If you are serious, you will accomplish as you planned, just do not lose focus. If for any reason you fall off track, get up and continue. You can find yourself a mentor to help you along the way. The person does not have to be with you physically but in your mind, to stay focused on that person, and if your desire is to be like him/her, you can be.

I have never met Robert Toru Kiyosaki personally but I have read his books, listened to his videos, and participated in his courses. I like his style, and I admire his accomplishments. He is a great mentor and a wonderful teacher, and he has earned a reputation for straight talk, irreverence and courage. When I say you do not have to meet your mentor personally, I mean it. You can find someone who you admire, someone who has the vision that you aspire. If you can meet with them go right ahead but if you cannot meet them personally do what I am doing; it can work.

Once you have that firm foundation, next comes the bricks and mortar to start construction. Based on the notes that you made in the foundation process you will now implement the construction. Utilize the tools in the various chapters of this book to start the construction. Take positive action based on the reason why you are investing in real estate. You can try different scenarios and see what works. There is a wealth of information in this book. You can also supplement this book with real estate workshops to get physical help. Remember, when in doubt just contact someone from 7figureretirement.com or TTTpropertiesinc.com; we are here to assist you to achieve your goal. You must take action in order to get off the ground. Once you close on the first investment property, the next one becomes easier.

It is a great idea to attend networking groups and workshops to meet like-minded people. You cannot do it alone, and no one will come and knock on your doors and offer assistance. It is a very good idea to mix and mingle but be careful who you are mixing and mingling with. Some workshops and/or networking groups are just for fun and people go week after week and month after month and achieve nothing. Try different ones until you hit the one that makes sense. You will know whether you are wasting time or if you are learning something. Depending on the outcome you stay or you move on. When you find the right one you will start feeling comfortable and confident and be encouraged to take action. You will also start using the same lingo, and understanding real estate terminology will become natural.

The house is now being built. Daily the structure is getting bigger and bigger and you are feeling a spirit of fulfillment. Yes, success is on the way; keep going.....you will meet new people who will be willing to share their experiences and offer assistance. You will tap into your power team that we talked about in Chapter 6. Now you are understanding the steps that you need to take before you go out in the field. You are doing your research via internet, real estate agents, mortgage brokers, etc. You are getting more comfortable with talking to other real estate investors and people in the business. It's okay; take your baby steps and eventually you will find yourself so confident that you will be assisting others. Keep thinking that you are building the house, and it takes many different tradesmen to complete it. In the same way you will rely on others from your power team to get the work done. If you do not have the money, don't let that stop you, remember, you can find joint venture partners. Develop your speaking skills and negotiation skills at the same time; they will do you good. Examine yourself and see what you are good at and complement your skill with someone who has other types of skill.

Once the house is complete, this is when you are ready to go and take action. You are feeling confident now, you will equip yourself with your property evaluator (which you will find at the end of this chapter) ready to evaluate properties for your portfolio. Remember, if you have no money, while you are going to workshops and networking meetings, you are marketing yourself with your other skills, preparing for joint venture partnership (they have the funds and you have got the skills/time).

Yes, it is that easy; just keep repeating the process and before you know it, you have achieved your 7 Figure Retirement!!!

Now for you seasoned real estate investors - As you read this book I am sure it will inspire you to higher achievements. You can use it to:

1. Encourage you to practice leveraging - the art of using other people's money to attain your wealth.
2. Create a better focus on buying more properties as well as managing the ones you already have in your portfolio.
3. Find additional creative ways to grow your portfolio.
4. Motivate you right out of your comfort zone and get you faster to your destination.
5. Use my property evaluator at the end of this chapter. This is a very important tool that will assist you in analyzing your property more

expeditiously and accurately, thus saving you time and money, which in turn will get you to your 7 Figure Retirement in an unbelievable amount of time.

PROPERTY EVALUATOR

Property Data:
Address:_____ City_____
Date Viewed:_____ Asking Price: $_____
Size(sw. ft.)_____ Year Built:_____
Repairs Required_____
Est. Cost $ _____
Owner's Name: _____ Tel: _____
Email/Fax: _____

Additional Notes:
Overall Rating: 1 2 3 4 5 - 5 (being the best)

Property Specific Questions:
1. What is the current state of the property?
2. Can you change the use of the property?
3. Can you buy it substantially below retail market value?
4. Can you substantially increase the current rents?
5. Can you do small renovations to substantially increase the value?

Area Economic Analysis:
1. Is there an overall increase in demand in the area?
2. Is the area growing faster than the provincial average?
3. Are there currently sales over list price in the area?
4. Are there active migration and immigration to the area?
5. Has the political leadership created a growth atmosphere?
6. Is it an area in transition, moving upwards in quality?
7. Is there a major transportation / infrastructure improvement occurring nearby?
8. Is it an area that will attract the baby boomers?
9. Is there a lot of speculative investment in the area?
10. Is the area's average income increasing faster than provincial average?

Based on the answers, do I approve this property?
Yes_____
No_____

The Property Evaluator is the weapon that I have been using in the last couple years to determine whether or not the property will fit my system. I have a vast number of them printed and I use one to analyze each property that I am interested in purchasing. If my end result is a "yes" I move forward with further due diligence. If my end result is a "No" I walk away, no questions asked. This little evaluator saves me a lot of time and of course time is money. This is a very useful tool; I encourage you to use it for each property that you have an interest in purchasing. Go For It - All the best!!

Chapter Eight
Finance Your Properties and
Make Money at the Same Time

Real estate investing requires money, but doesn't specify whose money. There are many ways to pay for investments and the list is only limited by your imagination and creativity. Here are some of the ways to pay for your real estate and make money at the same time:

1. All Cash – If you have the cash, buying property with no mortgage attached can be a very stable and safe return on your money. While the returns may not be as great as when using leverage (like a mortgage), the security is often worth it for many investors. Owning a property mortgage-free also enables you to sell on contract whenever you'd like.

2. Seller Financing – How Does Seller Financing Work? Seller financing is just what it sounds like; instead of the buyer getting a loan from the bank, the person selling the house lends the buyer the money for the purchase.

If a seller owns a property free-and-clear (no mortgage), they often times will be willing to finance the sale themselves. This enables you to buy a property without the hassle and cost of going through a bank or other lending institution. This is often an excellent way to acquire larger apartment complexes or commercial buildings, as the owners may want to continue receiving an income but not want the hassle of dealing with tenants. In this case the buyer and seller would execute a real estate contract providing an interest rate, repayment schedule and consequences of default. The buyer sends his monthly mortgage payment to the seller, who gets to earn interest on the loan, perhaps at a higher rate than he could get elsewhere.

Seller financing arrangements are often for a short term, such as five years, with a balloon payment due at the end. The idea is that the buyer will be able to refinance before then. Of course, arrangements like this can seriously backfire if you're not careful. Seller financing tends to be more common in markets where mortgages are hard to come by.

Would a Seller Offer Financing?

A home seller might be willing to offer financing for a number of reasons:

- to minimize carrying costs while waiting to find the perfect buyer and get a deal done quickly
- to distinguish the property from other listings and get it sold faster, especially in a down market
- to increase the possibility of garnering the home's full asking price
- to get a down payment to buy another property
- to pay down debt
- to ditch the monthly expense associated with owning the house

In other words, seller financing doesn't just benefit buyers who don't qualify for (or don't want) traditional financing. It also benefits sellers, especially those who are particularly motivated to sell their homes.

Advantages for Buyers

Seller financing has many advantages for buyers:

1. The closing process can be faster. Prudent buyers and lenders will always use the closing period to perform their due diligence. However with seller financing, the closing process can be faster. Some sellers claim that the reason for this is because there is no waiting for the bank's loan officer, underwriter and legal department to clear the file - a process that in districts easily stretches to several weeks.

2. Closing costs are also lower with seller financing because they can get in the home for less money. They do not have to pay the bank fees and appraisal costs.

3. The down payment amount can be extremely flexible. Instead of having to meet a bank or government-mandated minimum, the down payment amount can be whatever the seller and buyer agree to. This does not necessarily mean that the seller will accept a down payment that is lower than what the buyer would be required to pay elsewhere, but it's always a possibility.

Disadvantages for Buyers

There are also a few potential problems to consider when investigating the option of using seller financing:

1. Buyers should expect to pay a higher interest rate than they would to a bank.
    Buyers will have to pay an interest rate that makes the seller want to lend them money over investing their money elsewhere.

2. Buyers will still have to prove that they are worthy borrowers. It's one thing if a buyer and seller just want to remove the bank from the equation. However, if a buyer doesn't qualify for a traditional mortgage, there might be a good reason for that - and a seller may not want to become that person's lender, either.

3. Buyers need to make sure the seller owns the house free and clear or that the seller's lender agrees to the seller financing transaction. Most mortgages have a 'due on sale' clause that prohibits the seller from selling the home without paying off the mortgage. So if a seller does owner financing and the mortgage company finds out, it will consider the home 'sold' and demand immediate payment of the debt in full, which allows the lender to foreclose.

3. 20% - 25% Down Conventional Investment Mortgage – This is the classic method for buying a real estate investment through a bank. Depending on your qualification and the size and type of the property, if you come up with 20 - 25% down payment the bank will finance the rest of the mortgage.

4. 05% - 20% Down Conventional Personal Mortgage – This is similar to the above method, but you can often get a better interest rate if the property is your primary residence. This works best for duplexes, triplexes, and four-plexes.

5. 5% / 3.5% Down CMHC/ FHA Mortgage – If the home is your primary residence, you can often use a CMHC/FHA government insured loan that requires (currently just 5% / 3.5% down payment. Again, this is only on your primary residence. This is applicable for single family homes up to four units.

6. 3.5% Down 203K FHA Remodel loan – The FHA also has a loan program for buyers who want to buy a property that needs work to fix it up. The minimum down payment is (currently) just 3.5% of the total loan amount, and you are allowed to borrow the costs associated with remodeling the home – both labor and material. This can be an excellent way to build substantial equity in a primary residence without needing to have a lot of money upfront.

7. 10% HomePath Investment Mortgage – These loan types are only available on Fannie-Mae backed bank REOs, but can allow an investor to purchase the home for just 10% down payment with other benefits.

8. Small Partnerships / Joint Venture Partnership – Partnerships are an excellent way to invest in real estate, where two parties (or more) join forces and bring their talents, resources, and experience to the table to make a profitable investment. Perhaps you don't have the cash to buy an investment but have the time and your friend has the cash but no time – you can join forces and help strengthen the deal and make good money.

Sophisticated real estate investors create joint venture (JV) relationships in order to build their real estate portfolios more quickly than they could on their own, while using little or no money of their own. One party brings the real estate expertise while the other brings the investment funds or ability to obtain financing.

Not having enough investment capital is the most common reason investors do not purchase all the real estate they require to create their dream. It is inevitable, at one time or another, investors (veteran and rookie alike) run into a short or long term capital drought. Unsophisticated investors allow this road bump to stop them in their tracks, while sophisticated investors find a solution...and that solution is found in developing joint ventures. This is where you can also use RRSPs. Read The RRSP Secret by Greg Habstritt where he explains all the rules.

For your Joint Venture to be successful you must have the following:

Foundation: Do not go in with your eyes closed; there is a right way and a wrong way to build and operate joint venture relationships. Each joint venture relationship has key fundamentals that are shared. In order to make your life easier, your job is to look for commonalities, not exceptions. Your job as an investor and joint venture partner is to simplify and systemize your JV transactions, make it as cookie-cutter as possible, then deal with the exceptions.

A System: There must be a support system. Each person in the joint venture must support and complement each other. For example, one can be the money partner, the other can be the sweat partner. There must be foundational fundamentals. Must be wealth attraction principles in order to attract partners. The system must state how and where to find joint ventures. Must state how the deal will be structured. Must be legal.

To construct a joint venture partnership agreement you can email 7figureretirement.com or contact a real estate lawyer who knows about joint venture partnership.

9. Real Estate Syndication – When multiple parties join forces to buy a property it is known as a real estate syndication. This is an excellent opportunity to purchase large properties such as apartment complexes, shopping malls, or warehouses. There are stricter laws governing syndication, so be sure to consult with a real estate lawyer.

10. Use a Home Equity Line of Credit (HELOC) – If you have significant equity in your own home, you can often get a line of credit based on that equity. That money can then be used to finance almost any purchase, including residential property. This is a great way to finance fix-and-flips or to get the money needed for a down payment on a larger purchase. A HELOC is generally very low interest, and can be variable.

11. Use a Home Equity Loan – Similar to the HELOC, the home equity loan is (usually) a fixed-rate second mortgage on your primary residence that you can use to purchase anything you'd like – including real estate.

12. Small Business Loans – Banks often will finance a line of credit or loan for small businesses- and this can include a real estate investment company. Many banks (especially small, local banks) will even tailor a loan program just for you that can help you finance properties.

13. Self-Directed RRSP – This is a very powerful investment strategy. There are two types of RRSP Mortgages depending on whom the RRSP holder lends to, namely, Arms Length Mortgage and Non-Arms Length Mortgage.

Non-Arms Length - involves lending to a blood relative such as mother, father, brother or sister. It requires that the RRSP mortgage be insured (such as CMHC, for example). This involves an appraisal and an insurance premium depending on the loan to value ratio (LTV ratio) and calculated on a sliding scale up to approximately 4% of the loan amount.

Arms Length - is lending to a non-relative and there is no insurance required. In both cases, the RRSP Mortgage has to be managed by a Trustee who charges a nominal set up fee of approximately $250 and a similar annual fee regardless of the mortgage amount. Now, here is the great news; the terms of the mortgage i.e. the interest rate, the term and expiry date, the payment frequency are all agreed to between the RRSP lender (YOU!) and RRSP borrower. A lawyer will then prepare the documentation and register the mortgage to protect the interest of the RRSP lender.

Just think of this scenario as you, the RRSP holder, lending your RRSP to someone and enjoying the benefits of the interest rather than the bank lending it and enjoying the benefits of the interest.

If you are interested, here are the general steps and how it works:

a. You transfer the desired amount from your RRSPs to a trustee. Note you are NOT collapsing the RRSPs. The trustee acts as an intermediary holding onto your RRSPs and awaiting further direction from you. (Some banks can offer this although B2B, a subsidiary of Laurentian Bank, offers this service, and Olympia Trust is a great trustee also.) The reason that a trustee is required and you are not permitted to just transfer the RRSP to your account is because the RRSPs have not yet been taxed and so the government wants to protect what it's eventually owed in taxes payable on your yet untaxed RRSPs.
b. You find a home buyer who requires financing or an existing homeowner who requires refinancing.
c. You and the borrower agree to the amount to be borrowed, the interest rate and other such repayment terms. Note, at this stage you will also conduct your own due diligence to assure yourself that the property warrants the amount you intend to lend.
d. The agreement is documented by both your lawyer and the borrower's lawyer.
e. Your lawyer transfers the RRSP fund to the borrower's lawyer and registers your interest on the property by way of a mortgage registration on the deed or title to the property. Note that the borrower pays all fees.

f. The trustee will take care of the administration of the mortgage making sure that the mortgage payments are correctly deposited to your RRSP account. At this point there's really nothing left for you to do.

The above is offered as an overview and there are a few more details that you need to concern yourself about, but in general it's a fairly straightforward process. For further information please contact us at 7figureretirement.com or tt&trealestateinvestments.com or a lawyer who is familiar with self-directed RRSPs. This is a great way to increase

14. Self-Directed IRA Investing – Similar to RRSP above, except this is specific to the United States whereas RRSPs are specific to Canada. Many people have IRAs, but few know that you can actually use your IRA to invest in real estate. Difficult economic times have spurred non-traditional methods to save for retirement, and many people are using a self-directed IRA to purchase non-traded assets like real estate.

15. Whole Life Insurance – This little-known strategy can actually have a significant impact on your real estate investing career. If you have a whole life insurance policy, talk to your insurance agent about how you can borrow money against it to invest in real estate.

16. Using Hard Money – Hard money lenders loan money based primarily on the loan-to-value of a property. While the points and fees can seem high, they are often the best method to quickly finance a property. Be sure to always have an exit strategy, as hard money loans are typically good for less than two years.

17. Using Private Money – If you have friends, relatives, neighbours, or others who are looking for a better interest rate than the 1% or so they get from a bank savings account, they may be interested in lending that money to you to finance your acquisition. Generally, private money is based off the relationship more than anything, but still secured by the loan-to-value of the deal. This is one of the best ways to finance real estate, but use caution when there are personal relationships involved.

Make Money When Selling Investment Properties

Selling properties can net you a lot of cash – but can also cost a lot in fees, commissions, and taxes. The following is a list of ways you can make money when you sell:

1. For Sale By Owner – In today's world of advanced technology, it is possible to sell a home without using a real estate agent. While I generally do not advocate this route, many investors have found success and significant cost savings by selling the home themselves.

2. Flat Fee Selling Agents – There are many companies out there that will list your property for a set fee (from $99 – $1000) plus the buyer's agent commission (2- 2.5% or higher in some places) rather than the typical 5-7% due on normal transactions. The effectiveness of this strategy largely depends on your market.

3. 1031 Exchanges – In the US, when it comes time to sell, you can often avoid paying taxes on your profit by reinvesting that profit into another similar investment. This is known as a 1031 exchange. There are strict rules that govern this transaction, so be sure to seek professional advice before embarking on this journey.

4. Become the Seller Agent – Getting your real estate license does not require that you become a real estate agent. Often times you can save thousands of dollars by listing the property yourself.

5. Carry A Contract – When you sell, you can often defer all the taxes due plus receive a monthly income by selling on contract to a worthy buyer. This can also enable you to get a premium price for the property. Be sure to collect a sizable upfront down payment and screen your buyers very carefully.

6. Carry a Second Mortgage – While more popular in the past, this method is still a viable option to help close a deal. You can sell a property but be willing to carry a "second mortgage" at a higher interest rate. For example, the buyer puts 20% down, the bank funds 70%, and you fund the remaining 10% with a second mortgage on the property and the list goes on and on.....

7. Notes – Investing in "notes" involves the buying and selling of paper mortgages. While not necessarily a "property type," notes can be bought, sold, mortgaged, and traded just like the properties they represent. Oftentimes an owner of a property may choose to offer financing and "carry the mortgage". In this case, a "note" would be created which spells out the terms of the contract. For example, an apartment owner decides to sell his property for one million dollars. He offers to carry the full note and the new buyer will make payments of 8% per year for thirty years, until the full one million dollars is paid off. If that owner suddenly needed to get the full balance of the loan, he might choose to sell that mortgage to a "note buyer" for a discount. That note buyer will then begin collecting the monthly payments and decide if they will keep the note or try to sell it for profit.

Make Money By Teaching/Sharing Information in Real Estate:

Finally, if you have experience in real estate investing you can make additional income by sharing the knowledge you have:

1. Consulting – If you are experienced in real estate investing, perhaps you can share your information, help others, and make a decent side income while doing it.

2. Blogging – Creating a blog and discussing your real estate adventures can be a good way to organize your thoughts, build relationships with other investors, share your knowledge, and even build your list of lenders or buyers.

3. Retirement Specialists – A retirement specialist is similar to a consultant, but focuses primarily on helping individuals invest in real estate to achieve their retirement goals.

4. Author – Many investors choose to share their knowledge through writing and publishing a book. With the emergence of Amazon and other e-book providers, this is becoming significantly easier to do for anyone with a computer and a love of writing.

5. Infomercials – If you really want to explode your investing reach, you can rent space on a television network to gain followers or sell an informational product.

6. Public Speaking – Teaching others through speeches can be a great way to build your investment business and share what you know, while establishing yourself as an expert in the field.

7. Podcasting – A relatively new medium, podcasting brings the ability to create a radio show down to a level where anyone with a computer and microphone can experience it.

8. Talking TV Head – If you're especially experienced and love being in front of a camera, television networks like CNN, Fox, or MSNBC may be interested in knowing your perspective on trends in real estate.

9. Full-scale Guru – Please… just don't.

10. Get Involved – if you need help do not be shy, contact anyone at 7figureretirement.com or tt&trealestateinvestments.com; we are here to help you. There are many success stories that we can share with you to encourage you - we want you to be the next 7 figure real estate guru.

That's it! these are some of the ways you can achieve your 7figureretirement and there are lots more but too many to mention in this book. Please contact us for further information - 7figureretirement.com or tt&tpropertiesinc.com!

Chapter Nine
Creating Wealth

To create wealth in real estate investing you must have (a) the mindset; (b) a system that works; (c) affiliation and (d) the ability to take action.

Mindset - In order to create financial wealth in real estate investing, you must believe in yourself, and know WHY you are investing in real estate. This can lead you to become a successful investor. You must have an attitude about becoming wealthy, and the ability to utilize financial information to create that wealth by investing in real estate. A very wealthy man in real estate investing - Robert Kiyosaki - teaches in his program that you cannot rely on academic instruction on financial information because it does not cover wealth creation. He further stresses that the lack of this knowledge causes successful people to remain in a career for a lifetime of living from paycheck to paycheck. The majority of wealthy people in the world have made their money in real estate.

Clearly, many who wish to be wealthy and financially secure gravitate towards real estate as a means to accommodate those desires. They know to "follow the money." So while it's understood that there is a strong correlation between real estate and wealth, what's less obvious is that the inclusion of a focused business mindset is what completes the formula. Wealth is the destination, real estate is the vehicle, and a determined, business minded way of thinking is the fuel. To possess a strong business mentality and approach is the element that ultimately enables successful investing.

Most people who have made their money entirely from investing in real estate did so with a serious "treat it as a business" attitude, which itself was driven by a healthy entrepreneurial spirit. Generating wealth and achieving financial security through real estate investing truly is a (big) business and must be addressed as such. If it was easy, anybody could and would do it. Most aren't willing to do what's necessary. Those who are, tend to prosper...

Successful investors (entrepreneurs) have a highly developed and activated desire to realize their goals and destinations. They don't allow outside forces to impede. They are open, they search for and embrace all sources of helpful information, are incredibly optimistic and devote whatever time necessary to perform all of the due diligence to support their aims and minimize risks. If there are weaknesses or certain areas where they lack knowledge, extra emphasis on those is applied. They seek wisdom from, work with and partner with those who've already succeeded. As the right work is being done, fear and comfort zones become non-factors and success becomes likely.

Real estate investing is not something that only wealthy people do. In many cases investing in real estate is how their wealth was created. It should not be treated as a hobby. It is serious business, and understanding that separates those who are currently wealthy, those about to become so, and the others…

Overcoming Fear - I am a believer in the Bible and 2 Timothy 1:7 states: "For God hath not given us the spirit of fear; but of power, and of love, and of a sound mind." When I started out my real estate investing - like most people - fear tried to overtake me; and I repeated this verse over and over, and fear soon became history. For those who do not believe in the Bible, take heart, be strong, and say with authority "get out of me fear" and it will go!

What is your fear? Fear of failure? What your friends might say, or what your family might say if you do not succeed? Being human, these negative thoughts could cross your mind but there are ways to overcome them. Just know that, if you believe that statement of fear you have set yourself up for failure. Do not live your life focusing on negative things you do not want to happen in your life; this will create a negative mindset. Instead, write down your goals and describe them in detail. Keep reading them over and over and believing that you can achieve them. The key to overcoming fear is believing in yourself and knowing that what you believe, you will achieve.

Again the Bible tells you in Habakkuk 2:2 (King James Version): The Lord said "write the vision, and make it plain upon tablets, that he may run that reads it. For the vision is yet for an appointed time but at the end it shall speak and not lie; though it tarry, wait for it, because it will surely come; it will not tarry." For those who do not read the Bible, this is simply saying that you should write the vision, believe in it and act upon it for it to materialize, and it will.

Do you have fear of losing money? This fear is more powerful than the promise of great wealth or cash flow, and is the reason why most people do not buy their first property. What some people do not realize is that to receive some sort of reward from real estate you have to risk something – whether time, effort or money. However, very few are willing to risk anything because they are afraid of making a mistake and so they never get started. By the time you are finished reading this book I hope you will overcome all of your fears.

You will never meet a rich person who has never lost money at some point in their life. Most people have the fear of losing money, but successful people will not allow fear or doubt to control their thoughts and emotions or diminish their positive mindset. Failures inspire winners to achieve more because they use the failures as educational tools to move forward; this is the secret to success.

To overcome fear of losing money in real estate investing you must build confidence and step out of your comfort zone and take risks. You need not do it alone but refer to your power team in Chapter 6 of this book and get all the help that you deem necessary - eventually the fear will disappear. Stay focused on your destination and not on the journey. Zero In On Your WHY - If your "Why?" is compelling enough, you will stick around to learn this business. The only people I know who have failed in the real estate business are those who think they can get rich quick without learning the business.

The number one reason I like real estate is that it gives me the flexibility to have complete control of my time. I do not have to sit in my office day after day pounding away, trying to earn a living. I can come and go as I please.

As a real estate investor or a deal finder, you set your business up like a python sets up a meal. Every few months, the python feeds. And so it is with your business. Every few months, you will make a deal or facilitate a deal. One deal can give you enough income to equal your yearly salary without the hassle of working the 2,080 hours the average person works to earn that salary, while some professionals work in excess of 3,000 hours per year.

Another reason I enjoy the real estate business is I can find time to give back to my community and my church. I can contribute financially or physically. When I was working full-time for a company I was complaining along with my peers. Whenever we wanted time off, which is earned vacation, we were always told that this is a black-out period - which means we could not get the time off. Thanks be to God, now I can take time out to visit my little angel - my first little 8 month old grand-daughter Ava Reese in Charlotte, N.C. She is such a beauty, dancing, laughing, singing and ready to do modeling when she is discovered, which will be soon. There is freedom in real estate investing when you follow my system.

What is your Why? Whatever it is, real estate investing is what should take effect in your life.   The more you think out of the box the bigger and faster your business will become. Real estate gives the security of a hard asset that's worth something substantial; just follow my system or contact me at 7figureretirement.com.

Could Your Why Be - you have been a single mother/father for quite a long time and you are having a difficult time rearing your child/children mentally and physically, which can be draining at times? These might be your favourite people in the world who have loved you from Day 1, and will continue to love you to the end. Would you like to have some money set aside to 1) go on vacation with them every year which is a win for all of you, 2) assist them with their education 3) help them purchase their car, and 4) contribute to the purchase of their first home to kick-start their adult lives?

Now That Your WHY Is Determined - We will look at the three main components for becoming a successful real estate investor. Surprisingly the main components are not money, education or luck:

Component #1 - Systems - This is the foundation on which your wealth will be built. It must be a system that has been utilized and proven to be effective in any geographical area, and focuses on the type of property in which you want to invest. The system that I have used over and over, both for my many clients and myself, which proved very effective is as stated in chapter 10. Since this system is effective there is no need to make any adjustments; just repeat it over and over.

Component #2- Affiliations - Surround yourself with the experts in your field and utilize their expertise to the best of your ability. Affiliation will move your business forward in a positive way if you connect with the right people. Associate yourself with experts from your power team as set out in this book. While they are helping you, you will be able to help them in one way or another and it will become a win-win situation for everyone.

Don't forget to give back to someone else at the same time as others are giving to you. Do not focus on money, or you will become exhausted by constantly running for the next deal. Work with your team members; they will be some of the people that you will need to be your affiliates. Always remember to focus on your destination and not the journey!

Component #3 - Take Action - This is the component that most do not want to hear or talk about - they get very nervous. I hope that once you have read this book, your fear of taking action will disappear. If you do not take action, you will get nowhere. I cannot stress this component enough. There are many people who have completed many real estate courses, spent thousands of dollars over many years, but took no action and achieved nothing. My proven action system in Chapter

7 is all that you need when it comes to taking action. This action system is all that I have used to successfully find, analyze and purchase an abundance of excellent real estate properties. If you are still nervous or in doubt, please contact us at www.7figureretirement.com or tttpropertiesinc.com and we will be happy to assist you. Most of us here are immigrants and we have all been utilizing this system successfully.

In order for you to achieve your real estate investing goals more easily you must know WHY you have these goals; really give it some thought. Knowing your WHYs makes it that much more meaningful, deserving, and fulfilling when you achieve them. Sure, it can be for your family, your dog, for mankind... but the number one reason you want to achieve your goals should be for YOU. When on an airplane, they always instruct you in an event of an emergency to put the oxygen mask on yourself first before helping others. How would you be able to help your loved ones and to give back to the world if you don't have the emotional and financial capacity to do so?

I am a real estate investor/entrepreneur, dedicated to securing you wealth through strategic real estate investment. My mission is to help you achieve financial freedom by creating enough passive income to eventually replace your working income, so that you can spend more time doing what you love with the people you care about. Bear in mind that when we speak of real estate investing we are not just investing in houses as one might imagine but one could invest in condos, town houses, semi-detached homes, single family homes, multi-family buildings, commercial buildings, strip plazas, malls, land and the list goes on and on.......

Another thing to bear in mind is - you do not have to do it alone. I am here to assist you initially until you get comfortable or I can assist you permanently if you so desire. I can also set you up with a Joint Venture partnership, which is discussed in chapter 8....

Financial Literacy - Financial literacy is vitally important because it contributes to the mindset you need to develop to be a successful investor. It includes your attitude about becoming wealthy and your ability to utilize financial information to create wealth by investing in real estate. Unfortunately, most academic instruction does not cover wealth creation or financial literacy, which has doomed many seemingly successful people with prestigious careers to a lifetime of living paycheck to paycheck.

For such people, their lifestyle tends to grow with their annual pay increase or bonus, but that's where it stops. They do not have the knowledge required to make their money start working for them. They are also unable to put in place a financial team to help. They have to work until retirement and hope that there is enough money to maintain their expected lifestyle throughout their golden years.

Although this is acceptable for most of the population, you are reading this because you do not accept it! You picked up this book because you want to get out of the rat race described by Robert Kiyosaki in *Rich Dad Poor Dad*.

At the end of the day, people who are still in that rat race may feel they have security and stability. However their livelihood is at the mercy of company management. Their future can be drastically affected by an economy where seemingly stable companies suddenly dissolve. People can find themselves suddenly unemployed and unable to maintain their lifestyle while searching for new employment. Jobs are constantly being off shored from your homeland.

The truly successful are never satisfied with the status quo of corporate security and stability; they continually push to take on the next challenge. They are people of action, willing to do whatever it takes to reach their personal financial goals. We are not suggesting there is anything wrong with being career oriented or focused on moving up in your company. However, it is equally important to build your personal asset base, thereby putting yourself in a strong economic position. Then you can support your lifestyle regardless of what happens in the nine-to-five world.

Recent studies on the baby-boomer generation reveal that many people choose to continue working rather than retire. There are several reasons for this, such as improved health or enjoyment of what they are doing. However, one of the main reasons is financial need. For many of these people, poverty is the reward for adult lives spent continuously in the workforce or raising children and managing a family.

The time to create a financial guide for your family and to start building long-term wealth is now. Ideally, you want your personal assets to continuously work on your behalf so that your income stream isn't dependent on putting in certain number of hours each workday. What you choose to do with your time is something you can control. That is true financial and physical freedom.

Scammers - It is important to note that real estate scammers are out there and this can rob you of your real estate wealth. There are investment seminars that may try and convince you to follow high risk investment strategies, such as borrowing huge sums of money to buy property. Others promote investments that involve lending money for no security - or with other risky terms. While investment advice can be legitimate and beneficial, it is important to look carefully at what an investment scheme or seminar is offering. Attending an expensive seminar or investing in the wrong kinds of scheme can be costly mistakes.

You could be invited to an investment seminar in a number of ways - you might receive a card drop in the mail, see an ad in a newspaper or magazine, or hear about it through word of mouth. The seminar may promise that a motivational speaker, an investment expert or even a self-made millionaire will give you advice on investing. While this could be very profitable, it often can be just outright fraud....do your homework.

There are some legitimate organizations out there; some are pricy, some are not too pricy and others are free. Some of the free ones are called "Meet-up". Meet-up is very popular; almost every city has one or more. These are very informal; most are offered after work so most people go in their work attire. You can find organizations and Meet-ups on the internet.

Where ever you go, whatever you do, be cautious. Give yourself time to digest what is offered, and seek independent advice.

This is how I create my wealth as an immigrant in this country and there is no need for you as an immigrant to reinvent the wheel. Follow on and be successful!

Chapter Ten
Exit Strategies

Exit Strategies – This is a common phrase you will hear in real estate investing. While at first it may seem important that you learn everything you can about real estate investing, in reality, it is best to focus on two things: an investment vehicle and a strategy for using that vehicle. This chapter is going to introduce you to some of the most popular investment vehicles, as well as the most common strategies for moving forward.

You might absolutely love some niches and strategies, while others might make you shudder. As an investor, you are able to get a full view of the many different choices available to you, and you can then choose the one(s) that you enjoy the most. Best of all, you don't need to choose them all. Learning how to successfully invest in real estate is about choosing one niche and becoming a master of it.

Remember: Once you know the niche you want to get started with, you will be able to narrow down your focus, become an expert, network with individuals within that niche, and begin building wealth by taking action and executing a plan of action.

- Different types of properties
- Choosing Your niche
- Choose your real estate investing strategies
- Buy and hold
- Flipping
- Wholesaling
- Moving on

Raw Land - Raw land is nothing more than basic earth. Land on its own can be improved to add value, and it can be leased or rented to create cash flow. Land can also be subdivided and sold for profit. Some investors choose to buy raw land with hopes (or plans) that someday the land will become much more valuable due to external developments like the construction of a freeway or from a development being built nearby.

Single Family Homes - Perhaps the most common investment for most first time investors is the single family home. Single family homes are relatively easy to rent, easy to sell, and easy to finance. That said, in many areas, the rents derived from single family rentals (SFRs) won't be sufficient to provide enough positive cash flow unless you have more than one unit.

Duplex/Triplex/Quads - Small multi-family properties (2-4 units) combine the financing and easy purchasing benefits of a single family home. Bought properly, these can cash flow quite well, and there is often less competition than what you would come across on single family homes. Best of all, these properties can serve as both a solid investment as well as a personal residence for the smart investor. Another perk of the small multi-family property is the ability to take advantage of "economies of scale," as only one loan is needed to secure the 2, 3, or 4 units in the property.

One of the things that makes these investments so appealing is that most banks look at small multi-family properties with four units or less with the same guidelines as a single family house, which can make qualifying for a loan much easier.

Many real estate investors overlook some of the most profitable investment properties because they don't understand how smaller properties can equal big profits. They get caught up in the "bigger is better" mentality and miss out on some of the most profitable investments right in their own backyards. Contrary to what some real estate gurus say, you don't have to buy multi-family properties of 100 units or more to make a big profit. Smaller multi-family properties can provide an investor some of the strongest investment opportunities if you know what you are looking for. You can find them everywhere, and often times can buy them for much higher immediate returns and at better purchase terms than larger properties.

Small Apartments - We define smaller multi-family properties as those having five to fifty apartments or units. This size of property can be a great fit for individual or a small group of investors. At this size, the income can adequately cover the expenses of the property and factor in management, debt service, and vacancy expenses.

Though the line between small and large apartments is not set in stone, most investors typically draw the line between small and large apartment buildings at around 50 units. These properties can be more difficult to finance than single family homes or 2-4 unit properties, as they rely on commercial lending standards instead of residential ones. That said, these properties often provide significant cash flow for the investor who can deal with the more management-intense nature of the properties. Additionally, competition is generally seen on a lower scale for this property type, as they are too small for large, professional REITs to invest in (see below), but too large for most novice real estate investors.

Instead of being priced based on comps, the value of these properties are based on the income they bring in. This creates a huge opportunity for adding value by increasing rent, decreasing expenses, and managing effectively. These properties are a great place to utilize on-site managers who manage and perform maintenance in exchange for free or decreased rent.

Large Apartments - This class of property -- large apartments -- refers to the large complexes you might see all across the country that often include pools, work-out rooms, full time staff, and high advertising budgets. These properties can cost many millions of dollars to purchase, but can produce stable returns with minimal personal involvement. Many large apartments are owned by "syndications," which are small groups of investors who pool their resources.

REITs - REIT stands for a Real Estate Investment Trust. In the most simplistic definition, a REIT is to a real estate property as a mutual fund is to a stock. A large number of individuals pool their funds together, forming a REIT, and allow the REIT to purchase large real estate investments, such as shopping malls, large apartment complexes, skyscrapers, or bulk amounts of single family homes. The REIT then distributes profits to individual investors. This is one of the most hands-off approaches to investing in real estate, but do not expect the returns found in hands-on investing. You can buy shares in a REIT via your stock account, and they often have a relatively high dividend payment.

Commercial Investments - Commercial investments can vary dramatically in size, style, and purpose, but ultimately involve a property that is leased to a business. Some commercial investors rent buildings to small local businesses, while others rent large spaces to supermarkets or big box megastores. While commercial properties often provide good cash flow and consistent payments, they also may carry with them much longer holding periods during times of vacancies; commercial property can often sit empty for many months or years. Unless you are starting from a very solid financial position, investing in commercial real estate is not recommended for beginners.

Mobile Homes - You can start investing in mobile homes with little money out of pocket. Whether it's a home in a mobile home park or on its own land, many of the strategies used in other types of real estate investing can be applied to mobile homes.

Tax Liens - When homeowners don't pay their taxes, the government (local, state, or federal) can foreclose and resell the property to investors for the amount of taxes owed. This can often mean incredibly inexpensive properties, but be sure to do your due diligence and don't just jump into this kind of investing unprepared. Tax lien sales are complicated transactions that require research, knowledge and experience.

A Summary of Your Real Estate Investment Niche Choices:

I have just outlined several different investment niches, or vehicles, that you can invest in to take you on your journey through real estate investing. When starting out, it's helpful to simply pick one (or, at most, two) niches to focus on and become a pro at that niche. You can always expand later as you get more experience and knowledge.

While you can use any of these investment vehicles in your career, you must next learn an investment strategy that you can apply to that niche. The next section will look at several different strategies that investors use to make money with the various niches already covered.

Making Money Using These Popular Investing Methods/strategies - Just as there are many property types, there are also many ways you can make money with those properties. Every deal is different and may require a different strategy, so it is best to get acquainted with as many of these methods/strategies as possible. The secret is finding one method/strategy that you love and can throw your heart and soul into. The following is a list of methods/strategies and many of the top places to find good deals and make money when you buy:

1. Fix and Flip Single Family Homes – We'll start with the obvious and most popular one. Buy a cheap home, fix it up, re-sell it at a profit.

2. Buy-N-Hold Single Family Homes – Another favourfavourite. Buy a home, rent it out, hold it for a significant length of time. During this time your tenant pays down the mortgage and you also enjoy the cash flow at the same time.

3. Wholesale Single Family Homes – A popular choice for beginners, wholesaling involves scouting your local area, and in some cases outside your area, finding great deals, putting those deals under contract to buy, and then "assigning"(selling) those deals to an investor for a fee.

4. Hybrid Fix-N-Hold for Single Family Homes – One of my personal favourites, this incorporates finding the good deal and remodeling the home from the fix-and-flip but the long term benefits of the buy-n-hold. Simply, a single family home is purchased for a low price during a low market, remodeled to force appreciation, and held until the market improves and sold. This method seeks to maximize the Return On Investment (ROI) while limiting the risk.

5. Wholesaling Apartment Buildings – Some investors make their entire living off wholesaling just one or two large apartment buildings per year. With the larger price comes less deals but much higher finder's fees.

6. Fix-and-Flip Large Apartment Buildings – From duplexes all the way to large complexes, there are many apartment buildings in need of a complete overhaul. The benefit of flipping apartments over single family homes is the ability to collect rent while the property is being marketed for resale.

7. Buy-N-Hold Large Apartments – Similar to the long term approach to single family homes, but on a much larger scale.

8. Hybrid Fix-and-Hold for Apartments – Find a low-cost apartment building needing help, fix it, then rent it until it is most advantageous to sell.

9. Turn-Key-Investing – This type of investment is similar to a fix-and-flipper, but seeks primarily to sell the remodeled properties to out-of-town individuals seeking a good place to keep their money moving. Often times turn-key companies also can handle the management and all other issues, making the investment truly passive for the purchasing investor.

10. Vacation Rentals – Buying a property in a vacation area and renting it out when you are not staying there is not only a great way to pay for your vacation home but also build equity in a location where prices go up (and down with more extreme force.

11. New Construction, Residential – Just like it sounds. The process of building a home with the intent of reselling it.

12. New Construction, Commercial – Like residential, but involving commercial places.

13. Cash Purchase, Sell on Contract – If you have the cash, you can buy properties and then immediately re-sell them to buyers who may not be able to conventionally qualify for a mortgage. You can carry the mortgage for as long as you'd like, or sell the note for cash in the future. Make sure to collect a large down payment when using this method.

14. International Real Estate Investing – You don't need to live where you invest (but it often does help a lot). Many investors choose to live wherever they like but invest where it makes the most sense – often overseas. While there are many challenges to this type of investing, there are also huge rewards to those who can effectively navigate the international waters.

15. Lease-Option Sandwich – Without actually owning the property, lease-options allow a person to gain control of a property by leasing it with a legal "option" to purchase the property at a specified price within a specified time period. Often times these properties can be re-"sold" using another lease option and the investor simply makes money being the "middle man."

16. Lease Option – As mentioned earlier, a lease-option (lease purchase) is a method used to control real estate without taking title. It is simply "renting" the property with the legal right to buy it later. This can be a good way to buy a property if your intent is to quickly sell it again later.

17. For Sale By Owners (FSBO) – Oftentimes, sellers will decide to save the costs of hiring a real estate agent to sell their home and sell it themselves with a sign or newspaper advertisement. These sellers can often times be excellent sources of finding good deals or seller-financed deals.

18. Buying REOs – REOs are bank-owned properties that were taken back in foreclosure. Oftentimes these properties can be picked up for significant discount, as a bank is often very willing to get the loan off their books. Additionally, there is no emotional attachment on the part of the bank. You can use any of the above-mentioned strategies to dispose of such property.

19. Auction at the Courthouse Steps – During the process of foreclosure, a home is generally brought to the courthouse steps to be sold to the highest bidder. If no one bids, the home goes back to the bank. Oftentimes, homes can be purchased for steep discounts using this method.

20. Buying in Pre-foreclosure – Sellers on the brink of losing their home can be very motivated to sell their home and save their credit. Many times, more is owed on the house than the house is worth. However, sometimes great deals can be found by weeding out a lot of bad deals.

21. Tax Liens – When homeowner's refuse to pay their taxes, the government can foreclose and resell the property. You've probably seen the "Pennies on the dollar" infomercials on late night television, but this method can be trickier than the gurus portray on TV...make sure you do your research on other balances that are owing on these properties.

22. Buying REOs – REOs are bank-owned properties that were taken back in foreclosure. Oftentimes these properties can be picked up for significant discount, as a bank is often very willing to get the loan off their books. Additionally, there is no emotional attachment on the part of the bank.

23. Short Sales – A bank will often take less than the loan amount on a property to save the hassle and costs of foreclosing. This means you can often get a great deal if you can wade through the red tape and long wait-times that short sales involve.

Make Money Using These Marketing Techniques:

Without proper marketing, you'll never make any money in real estate. Whether renting, selling, buying, or any other activity, these techniques will help you find the solutions to the issues you face.

1. Real Estate Agents/Brokers – Finding a good real estate agent/broker is essential to enjoying a painless real estate transaction. The saying is "20% of the agents do 80% of the business," and it is true. The question is how can you find a good real estate agent? The best agent for you doesn't necessarily work at the largest brokerage, close the most transactions or make the most money. The best agent for you is an experienced professional who will listen to you, conduct himself/herself in an ethical manner, and knows your market. Do your research and/or get referrals.

2. Newspapers – The classic way of advertising still is one of the best, if you can afford it.

3. Craigslist / Kijiji Ads – Craigslist & Kijiji are free, easy to use, and taking over the marketing from newspapers across the country. If you have not used these sites yet, please do so.

4. Websites – Websites today are very inexpensive and easy to create. You have no excuse to at least have a Facebook page, LinkedIn, Twitter or Google+ page.

5. Bandit Signs – You've seen them before – those rectangular, often hand-written signs, that advertise "we buy houses" or a variety of other sales information. While tacky and well used, this method is still one of the best ways to market your business. (Be aware that they are illegal in many, if not most areas.)

6. Direct Mail – This old school method of finding leads still works today. Sending out a massive amount of letters, especially to your defined target market, is a great way to get calls and weed through deals.

7. PPC Marketing – PPC (short for Pay Per Click) marketing is the process of soliciting business online through companies like Google, Facebook, Bing, and Others. The beauty of PPC marketing is that you only pay when an ad is clicked on – thus you only pay when an ad works.

 8. Business Cards – If you don't have business cards, you are leaving a lot of money on the table. Hand out business cards to every person you meet and you'll be surprised at how quickly your business grows.

Word of Mouth – Despite all the technology we have today, nothing will ever come close to the effectiveness of word-of-mouth advertising. Make Money By Lending Money:

Lending money is one of the oldest, and most profitable, businesses on the face of the earth. As one famous person once said, "You aren't making money until your money is making money."

Hard Money Lender – A hard money lender is a person who lends money for the acquisition and/or improvements to an investment property – based almost entirely off how good the deal is. If you are looking for a way to earn significant returns on your money without needing to actually own the property, consider becoming a hard money lender.

Conclusion

As I come to the end of this book, I would like to encourage all you immigrants out there to create wealth with real estate. Just bear in mind that it is not by your financial status, education, social status, ethnicity, or any of those things that will draw you closer to your financial goal. Every one of us has tremendous potential to achieve the success and wealth of our dreams. Set goals, each one should be higher than the previous, dream big and cultivate the mindset that is the foundation of your success. I will set out in the next paragraph, what has helped me, as an immigrant, to create wealth, and hope that you can use the same strategies to be a successful real estate entrepreneur.

Find your real estate niche, one that you are passionate about, and let it drive you to the 7 Figure Retirement. Begin today by asking yourself "What is my "WHY" for wanting to invest in real estate?" Clearly identify and define your goals, WRITE them down and WORK towards them. Use your Property Evaluator for every property that you have an interest to purchase. Work with my strategies in this book. Set timelines and milestones and track your progress while you stay motivated. If an obstacle comes your way, do not be discouraged; find a way to overcome it - there will be several ways to overcome obstacles - do NOT give up!

Some real estate properties will appreciate immediately while others might appreciate slowly. The important thing is, you should make money on the buy. What that means is, if the current market value for the property is $400,000 and you pay $350,000 you are making $50,000 at the time of buying, so you are ahead at the time of purchase. Make sure also that the property is going to cash flow if you are holding it for long term wealth. What that means is, once you pay all of your expenses at the end of the month, there should be cash left over for you. The more cash you have at the end, the better the investment.

It is an excellent choice to become a successful real estate entrepreneur. Pursue your success by thinking big and staying on track. This is a business and should be treated as such. Treat your tenants well; treat them with respect and listen to their concerns. They are paying for your real estate, they are putting cash in your pockets, they are helping you to achieve your 7 Figure Retirement goal. If there is a deficiency in the property and they call you, immediately attend to their concerns. Do semi-annually check inside the properties to make sure they are kept in order. It is very important to have a good working relationship. If you look around you, most of our jobs are being outsourced. Companies are scaling down and pressuring one person to do two, three or even four jobs. You have made the right choice.

Invest in your knowledge. Keep up to date with changes in the fundamentals of real estate investing. Continue to do relevant courses, network with like minded people, attend seminars, workshop, read books and newspapers, speak to other investors and people on your power team.

Be encouraged, do not let anyone tell you that because you are an immigrant you cannot achieve 7 Figure Retirement, it is possible, use my book and show them how.

I like Zig Ziglar; he encourages me, so let him encourage you also. Here are some of his quotes:

1. Your attitude, not your aptitude, will determine your altitude.

2. The foundation stones for a balanced success are honesty, character, integrity, faith, love and loyalty.

3. Be grateful for what you have and stop complaining - it bores everybody else, does you no good, and doesn't solve any problems.

4. You cannot climb the ladder of success dressed in the costume of failure.

5. It was character that got us out of bed, commitment that moved us into action, and discipline that enabled us to follow through.

5. You were born to win, but to be a winner, you must plan to win, prepare to win and expect to win.

6. I have always said that everyone is in sales. Maybe you don't hold the title of salesperson, but if the business you are in requires you to deal with people, you, my friend, are in sales.

Real Estate Abbreviations

There is a huge amount of vocabulary that is used by the real estate industry, and many terms are often abbreviated in day to day discussions, on contracts and agreements, and by real estate agents. Here are some of the abbreviations and what they really mean:

ARV	After-Repaired Value
COO or COFO	Certificate of Occupancy
CMA	Comparative Market Analysis
COCR or CCR	Cash on Cash Return
COF	Cost of Funds
CRE	Creative Real Estate
CRE	Commercial Real Estate
DCR / DSCR / DSR	Debt Service Coverage Ratio
DTI	Debt to Income Ratio
FHA	Federal Housing Administration
FMR	Fair Market Rent
FMV	Fair Market Value
FSBO	For Sale by Owner
GRM	Gross Rent Multiplier
HML	Hard Money Lender
HOA	Homeowners Association
HUD	Housing and Urban Development
IRA	Individual Retirement Account
IRR	Internal Rate of Return
JV	Joint Venture
L/O	Lease Option
LLC	Limited Liability Company
LLP	Limited Liability Partnership
LTV	Loan to Value
MAO	Maximum Allowable Offer
MLS	Multiple Listing Service

NNN	Triple Net Lease
NOI	Net Operating Income
NOO	Non-Owner Occupied
OO	Owner Occupied
O/F	Owner Finance
P&S	Purchase and Sale
PCF	Price to Cash Flow (ratio)
PITI	Principal, Interest, Taxes and Insurance
PUD	Planned Unit Development
REI	Real Estate Investing
REIA	Real Estate Investors Association
REO	Real Estate Owned
ROI	Return On Investment
RTO	Rent to Own
SFH	Single Family House
SFR	Single Family Residence

Glossary

Abstract Of Title
A written history of the title to a parcel of real estate as recorded in a Land Registry Office.

Accrued Interest
Interest that has accumulated unpaid since the last payment date.

Adjustment Date
The date regarded as the official beginning of a mortgage.

Affidavit
A statement of declaration in writing and sworn or affirmed before an authorized individual, such as a notary public.

Agency
A relationship that arises out of a contract, where an agent is authorized by a principal to engage in certain acts, usually in dealing with one or more third parties.

Agreement of Purchase and Sale
A written contract to buy property in which the purchaser and vendor agree to sell upon terms and conditions as set forth in the agreement.

Alienation Clause
This is a clause that enables the mortgagee to demand payment of the outstanding balance including interest upon sale or transfer of title (also known as a "due-on-sale" clause).

Amortization
The gradual retirement of a debt my means of partial payments of the principal at regular intervals.

Appreciation
The increase in value of a property over time; it is influenced by many factors such as inflation, the economics of supply and demand and capital improvements.

Asset
In real estate, this is property under ownership that has value.

Balance Sheet
It provides a snapshot of a company's financial position. The assets appear on the left, listed in the order in which they can be converted into cash. Liabilities appear on the right in the order they must be liquidated.

Balance Due on Completion
The amount of money a purchaser will be required to pay to the vendor to complete the purchase after all adjustments have been made.

Balloon Payment
This is a final mortgage payment at the end of the term that pays off the outstanding loan in full. the amount of money (principal) required to discharge a mortgage at maturity.

Bird Dog
a person who looks for properties that fit your guidelines and brings them to you for a fee.

Blanket Mortgage
A single registered document that encumbers more than one property.

Blended Payment
Equal payments consisting of both principal and interest, paid regularly during the term of the mortgage.

Canada Mortgage and Housing Corporation (CMHC)
A Canadian Crown Corporation that administers the National Housing Act. CMHC services include the insuring of high-ratio mortgage loans for lenders.

CAP
Refers to a maximum interest rate increase for a mortgage.

Capital
Assets such as a sum of money that can be used to acquire or product other assets.

Cash Flow
The difference of cash revenues less cash outlays over a given period of time (excluding non-cash expenses).

Comparables
Data about properties that are comparable in type and size to the one that is of interest to a buyer or a seller. The information can consist of previously sold properties as well as current listings.

Damages
Compensation or indemnity for loss owing to breach of contract.

Debt Service
The amount of principal and interest payments made under a mortgage.

Debt Service Ratio
Measurement of debt payments to gross household income.

Default
Failure to abide by the terms of a mortgage loan agreement.

Due Diligence
A number of concepts involving the investigation of a business or person, or the performance of an act to specified standards.

Economic Depreciation
Loss in value of property due to external influences related to the property, i.e. not controlled by the owner.

Equity
The difference between the market value of the property and the claims held against it.

Estate
The degree, quantity, nature and extent of interest that a person has in real property.

First Mortgage
the mortgage agreement that has first claim on the property in the event of default.

Foreclosure
When an owner does not make the mortgage payments and therefore defaults on a mortgage contract, the lender will repossess the property.

Gross Rent Multiplier
Method of appraising the fair market value of a property by multiplying the gross rents by a factor that varies according to the type and location of the property.

Gross Debt Service
The percentage of gross annual income required to cover payments associated with housing.

High Ratio Mortgage
A mortgage loan that exceeds 75 percent of the lending value of the property and must be insured against default of payment.

Highest and Best Use
this refers to the use of land that would most likely produce the greatest net return over a given time.

Internal Rate of Return (IRR)
The gain or loss of an investment over a specified period, expressed as a percentage.

Irrevocable
Incapable of being recalled or revoked; unchangeable, unalterable.

Joint Tenancy
Ownership of land by two or more persons whereby, on the death of one, the survivor or survivors take the whole estate.

Joint Venture
The partnership between two or more parties for the purpose of acquiring and developing real estate.

Leasehold Mortgage
A mortgage given by a lessee on the security of the leasehold interest in the land.

Leverage
Strategic use of borrowed capital to increase the potential return of an investment.

Lien
The claim placed by a creditor on a piece of real estate to ensure the payment of a debt.

Market Value
The highest price estimated in terms of money that a property will bring if exposed for sale in the open market.

Net Operating Income (NOI)
The balance remaining after deduction of operating expenses from gross receipts and gross rental but not including the deducting of debt service on mortgages.

Net Worth
A person's total financial worth, determined by subtracting total liabilities from total assets.

Open-End Mortgage
A mortgage under which the lender has the option of advancing more funds where, for example the value of the property is anticipated to increase.

Option
A right given by the owner of a property to another (for valuable consideration) to buy a certain property within a limited time at an agreed price, an option holder who does not buy at or within the specified period loses the deposit and the agreement is cancelled.

Portfolio
The investment holdings of an investor or investment company.

Power Of Sale
The right of a mortgage to force the sale of the property without judicial proceedings should default occur.

Principal
The amount originally invested or loaned. Interest rates and returns are calculated based on this amount.

Quit Claim Deed
A general release of all claims or rights to a parcel of land.

Refinance
To pay off (discharge) a mortgage and other registered encumbrances by arranging a new mortgage.

Return On Investment (ROI)
The level of profit expected from the investment.

Right
The interest one has in a piece of property, i.e. a claim or title enforceable by law.

Sandwich Lease
A lease in which the "sandwich party" is the lessee of one party and the lesser to another. Usually, the owner of the sandwich lease is neither the fee owner nor the user of the property.

Statute
A law established by an act of the legislature.

Sweat Equity
Labor used to build or improve a property and increase its equity.

Tangible Asset
A physical asset with intrinsic value, such as land or real estate.

Tax Lien
A lien imposed by a taxing authority on real estate for failure to pay taxes within the time required by law.

Tenure
A system of land holdings for a temporary time period.

Title Insurance
A policy that insures the lender and purchaser against loss due to a flaw in the title of property held as collateral for a mortgage.

Vendor Take Back (VTB)
Where the seller will take back a portion of the mortgage, creating a secondary lien on the property.

Acknowledgements

First and foremost, I must say thanks to God, my heavenly Father from whom all blessings flow. Without Him I could never have achieved this book. Thanks to my late mother also who from a young age taught me to believe in myself and also that with God all things are possible. Love you always mom.

To my dear husband of many years, Fitzbert Henriques, I would like to say thanks for your continuous belief in me, your constant support and the long hours that you invested, working around the house while I pursue my dreams and spend time building my real estate investment business. I feel so inarticulate in finding words to thank you enough for your unwavering patience, humility and unconditional love. I would also like to make a public declaration that you are the best husband and father that God created. Thank you so very much.

To my three daughters, Dr. Trecia Henriques (medical), Dr. Tracy Henriques (toxicologist) and Attorney Tanielle Henriques-Campbell - thanks a million for your sincere support and encouragement. I was always encouraging you to write a book because there is so much that you could write about. Instead you told me to go ahead because you realized that real estate investing is my passion and you told me to let it out - so I did. You are the best daughters that a mother could ever ask for. Thank you so much for your input ladies, and to you Tanielle - even though you are juggling work, husband and our little 8 month old angel Ava Reese, you still find time to call me night after night to find out if I am finished. Thank you; now I am. Thanks to you also, BJ (Tanielle's husband) - you are wonderful, the son that I was not able to give birth to, but I got you through marriage. May God continue to prosper you for your kind and passionate heart.

To my two sisters Miriam Samuel and Myrtle Ennis, words cannot express my gratitude to you over the years. Sisters like you are hard to find but I thank God for you. You are always caring for me, your youngest sister, always giving me and encouraging me - thank you very much.

To my nieces - thanks for your assistance in more ways than one, especially you Jacqueline Jaghai, always giving and making sure that others are okay. Your kindness will return to you 100 fold. To the rest of my immediate and extended family including my in-laws, thank you for all the help that you gave me, much appreciated.

To my pastor, Dr. Pat Francis of Kingdom Covenant Ministries, Mississauga, Ontario; Pastor thank you for the time you spend, the hours you gladly give, for your shepherding, leading on the upward path, sharing of the gift God gave you to bless us with His word, unfolding of God's perfect way, the only way to live. I thank God for you as I lift you up in prayer.

To my telephone prayer partners, Grace Henry and Shirley Rodney; thank God for the day when we decided to form this prayer shield, calling and connecting at 6.00a.m. every morning. God is truly blessing us. Let us continue to do His will and Grace, thanks for all the extra push that you gave me so that I could keep on schedule. I would like to thank my Monday Night Prayer Group also for their prayers and support. I love you all.

To all my friends, including Dolly Guinness, you are a great inspiration to me and I thank you very much. There are so many people who have blessed me in one way or another, if I forget to name you please forgive me and accept my apologies, I love you all!

And last, but definitely not least, to my mentor, Julie Broad, who came into my life at such an opportune time, I thank you. You are such an inspiration, and a goal setter. If I only had you earlier I would have achieved so much more, but I thank God that I met you - one of

Amazon's best sellers and CEO of RevNYou, Julie, you are great, and I can only wonder how you do it. May God bless you abundantly as you continue to mentor others into their destiny.

Thanks to everyone!!

About the Author

Lurline Henriques left Jamaica at the age of 21 in search of more opportunities. While in Canada she puts herself through school, raising three professional daughters, building a great career with the Federal Government and becoming a successful real estate investor. Today, as she settles in to retire with a real estate portfolio worth over seven figures, she's helping you set yourself up for a wealthy retirement at any age. Lurline volunteers with Kingdom Covenant Ministries, Junior Achievement of Central Ontario, Canadian Diabetes Society, is a past member of Real Estate Investment Network, Rock Star Inner Circle, and a current member of Toastmasters, Toronto Board of Trade and several Meet Up Groups.